IN DOGGED LOYALTY

John F. Deane

In Dogged Loyalty

THE RELIGION OF POETRY: THE POETRY OF RELIGION

the columba press

First published in 2006 by
the columba press
55A Spruce Avenue, Stillorgan Industrial Park,
Blackrock, Co Dublin

Cover by Bill Bolger
Origination by The Columba Press
Printed in Ireland by ColourBooks Ltd, Dublin

ISBN 1 85607 534 6

Acknowledgements
Some of these essays, or versions of them, have been published in
The Irish Times,
Sources, ed. Marie Heaney, (Town House Dublin, 1999)
Faith and the Hungry Grass, ed. Enda McDonagh, (Columba Press 1990)
The Hero, Home, John F. Deane, (Dedalus Press 2001)
Manhandling the Deity, John F. Deane, (Carcanet Press, 2003)
The Furrow
and presented as a lecture at the Merriman Summer School, 2005
The author and publishers gratefully acknowledge the permission of
the following to use poems which are in their copyright: Bloodaxe
Books for *Moorland, Folk Tale* and *No Time,* all by R. S. Thomas: Pádraig
J. Daly for his poems *Sagart I, Encounter, Complaint, Last Dreamers, The
List* and *Trinity*; Thomas Kinsella for his poem *Hen Woman.*

Table of Contents

You

I am sea-born, and sea-inclined; islanded
on this earth, dragged each-which-way, and tidal;

senses shifting as the sands shift, my soul
flotsam. Prisoned in time, and you, love,

are eternity, you are the current in my depths,
my promised shore. And when I part from you,

taking my words to dry, sophisticated places, I am
tugged towards you, sweet desperation, this underwater storm.
John F. Deane

God's Grandeur:

On Writing Religious Poetry in a Secular age

If I say 'God', do you blush and turn away? If I say 'sacrament, heaven, angelus ...' and if I mutter 'poetry', do you giggle in embarrassment? Religion has become the new pornography; religious poetry the new lunacy. The late Dermot Morgan took joy in mimicking the priest whose language was riddled with cliché; the Monty Python team took riotous pleasure in their 'Life of Brian', in parodying sundry sermons and 'Oh Lordisms!' When a language becomes so clichéd that it loses relevance, what is needed to begin a revival is a series of ironic and iconoclastic works. It always interested me to know that in French the *Pater* begins with *'Notre père qui es aux cieux ...'* in other words using the 'tu' familiar form of the verb, whereas the *Ave* begins with *'Je vous salue, Marie ...'* using the polite form. And just the other day I heard someone in church behind me say the *Pater* like this, 'Our Father who are in heaven, hallowed be your name, your kingdom come ...' and later on sing out 'Hail Mary full of grace the Lord is with thee ...' Words are central to our thinking, our traditions and our behaviour. The old hymns: *Holy God we praise Thy name ..., Hail Queen of Heaven the ocean star ...* have lost their savour. If they are being replaced by platitudinous and gratuitously 'modern' non-hymns that is nobody's fault but time's.

It is the context and culture of one's early years that define the form of the God to whom one is introduced. My life on Achill Island was one of freedom, exhilaration, and exultation in the physical beauty of that place. The fact that a child is unconscious of such influences and emotions is immaterial: the egg-yolk gold of blossoming furze bushes, the fuchsia-lined narrow roadways where the blood-red flowers would toss themselves against your face as you cycled by, the awesome and monstrous cliffs that faced away onto the empty Atlantic Ocean ... all of that and so much more entered into my being and has remained a source of solace and of grace. And a God slipped in alongside, though it has taken me many decades to put a name to that God. I began with a Jesus of morne misery, a severe minister of don'ts and do's, of pain and sorrow, of eyes that squinted at you as they followed you everywhere. I have turned to poetry to recover a Jesus of more relevance and truth.

It has been written that the artist is the isolated conscience who stands for the universal conscience, over against the mass mind. If this is so then the artist's place is solitude, his being in the midst of people ought to remind mankind of its deep capacity for peace, maturity and hope. We have been led to believe that there is a certain kind of 'insanity' that touches an imaginative spring to keep the world from deserts of barbarism and destruction; unfortunately we are witnesses to new barbarism in our time, a barbarism perpetrated by those half the world considers 'sane'. As I grew into adulthood I became aware that the artist was seen as someone who stood challenging the Christian ethos (in our case the sad bleakness of Catholicism) and manifesting an alternative and 'liberated' non-faith; now I feel, with our secular society so much at odds with deep human and universal rights and yearnings, it is the Christian artist who stands nonconformist rebel, challenge to such secularism. As Thomas Merton wrote in *Raids on the Unspeakable*, 'Poetry is the flowering of ordinary possibilities. It is the fruit of ordinary and natural choice ... We are the children of the Unknown. We are the ministers of silence that is needed to cure all victims of absurdity who lie dying of a contrived joy. Let us then recognise ourselves for who we are: dervishes mad with secret therapeutic love which cannot be bought or sold, and which the politician fears more than violent revolution, for violence changes nothing. But love changes everything.' These days I'm not so sure that politicians fear the work of poets – it is much easier to ignore such work as poets do not get time and space to present their work properly, and poets who take religion as their theme are generally safely ignored.

We move in a world where politicians, sheen-suited and sheen-faced, glide on a sheened surface, under which truth lies drowning; fiction writers churn out the most blithe and blanc-mange-wobbly yarns to keep the mind from reality, and book-shops sell them by the millions. All of this gratefully eschews the value that aesthetic experience brings to human living, it settles for the least, leaving us bereft. If poetry (and the same applies to fiction) is reduced to serving the needs of amusement, the loss to the human spirit is immense. Poetry pushes experiences that are inaccessible to rational disquisition; it works to lift the rationalist into the shocking position of dealing with things that go bump beyond the thin partition of human reasoning. Rilke, for in-stance, who was indeed no easy 'orthodox' believer, tried through his poetry to create a faith by which he could live; he stands as emblem of the loneliness of the modern man, not urg-ing retreat into the cave of other-worldliness but calling out, one individual, in opposition to the churning together of the masses and the sheened civilisation of machines and ideologues. For him, the 'angels' hold true meaning yet are so far removed from human experience that he can say (in the 'First Elegy'):

> beauty is nothing
> But the beginning of terror, which we can barely endure;
> We dwell in wonder because it calmly disdains
> To annihilate us. Every angel is terrible.

As Elizabeth Jennings wrote in *Every Changing Shape*: 'the tension in these great elegies lies in the implicit yet unacknowl-edged belief that reality exists autonomously in an area of exper-ience that only poetry can penetrate'. And there is Galway Kinnell:

> ... poetry sings past even the sadness
> that begins it ...

And again he writes:

> When the song goes, silence replaces it
> inside the bones.

I see the need, then, for poetry, and I see how it is ignored. Further, I see the need for 'religious' poetry and know that it is even more ignored. It must be said, in its immediate defence, that great religious poetry is non-aligned. Since Constantine had his vision that he would conquer the world under the sign of the cross, the proselytising urge has been dominant. The journeys undertaken by the Popes into far-flung countries manifest that same desire, in a church that is losing its hold on power. However, in the 1980s, Pope John Paul II publicly reprimanded the supreme Nicaraguan poet, Ernesto Cardenal, for promoting a liberation theology, a religion that took account of the poor and marginalised, that the prelate found divergent from Roman Catholicism. Cardenal himself had worked tirelessly for the liberation of his people, his poetry, a religious poetry, being one of the strongest weapons he wielded. Cardenal himself views his poetry as a medium for his message of the transformation of the old, unbalanced order into a new and more just society in which utopian dreams and Christian values can become one. The rebuke not only alienated a great poet from the church, but alienated many more around the world who saw the Pope on the side of power and the old order. How often has the name of religion been used for political purposes! Islam appears to be gaining much ground in its domination of the lives of men; how far does Christianity continue to dominate our lives? Indeed, the question may be asked if Christianity truly ever did dominate our living. The strength of religious poetry may well offer a clue to an answer. In our day the very language and imagery of Christian living appear to have lost a great deal of their force.

By 'religious poetry' I mean poetry that delves into questions of transcendence and the soul's longing for immortality, rather than devotional hymns or bland statements of faith. For those of us who have tried to cling to some meaningful wisps of faith from that Catholic past, the problem is how to revive and renew the old, jaded language and imagery. The deepest springs of religious poetry are not in any way allied to preaching; if origin and end of inspiration produce a religious poem then it will be in harmony with all truth, mystical, moral, metaphysical and will be the richer for all that. Dannie Abse wished 'to become the music while the music lasts'; to be a sparkle on the frozen lake for as long as the sun shines over it. A poem is in itself an argument against nothingness. It is my belief that a good religious poem is the final argument against nothingness. In our time the corrosion of the religious imagination is therefore the more depressing.

To be a Christian poet is to try and raise a voice against injustice because the heart loves the world the way God loves it. The imagination sees how it should flourish; when this flourishing collides with the social arrangements people make at one another's expense or at the expense of the earth, the poet is moved to speak out and act in service of the reign of God, thus creating possibilities for resistance and resurrection. The religious poem insists still on the certainty of man's insignificance in the immensity of this hostile universe, yet retains at least the questioning hope of transcendence.

God is killed, not by aggression, but by indifference. Poetry is murdered in the same way. It is sad to see how religious poetry is dismissed by the facile use of the all-cloaking word 'mystical'. And it is sad to see how so much Christian, particularly Catholic, writing seemed allied to the right. I urge the pleasures of great religious poetry; I point to its relevant probing; I see how poetry is a way of crossing the abyss between one world into another, this other perhaps being the one that is most real, less fragmented than the one we live in.

T. S. Eliot wrote: 'real poetry survives not only a change of popular opinion but the complete extinction of interest in the issues with which the poet was passionately concerned.' If a nation ceases to produce great writers, especially great poets, the language and culture will deteriorate. By affecting the language you affect the sensibility of a nation. The possibility of regaining a religious poetic received impetus with the work of writers like Eliot, like R. S. Thomas, like Czeslaw Milosz, who wrote, in *A Year of the Hunter*: 'The mainstay of the Catholic Church appears to be the faithful who refrain from questioning, either because it's of no interest to them or because they have surrounded themselves beforehand with an impregnable barrier.' Serious questioners, he believed, inevitably become heretics. 'Poetry's separation from religion has always strengthened my conviction that the erosion of the cosmic-religious imagination is not an illusion and that the vast expanses of the planet that are falling away from Christianity are the external correlative of this erosion.'

I wonder if the size, shape and magnificence of our churches has some bearing on our view of ourselves in relation to God? The high forests of the Gothic cathedrals, man's smallness; Gallarus oratory, the soul naked and cramped before God with the might of the sea just outside; the bland unartistic walls of the village church, and the sterile interior, the sterile soul. Our popular fiction mimics this sterility. Religious poetry says that there is more than this febrile search for the fast lane, the life of progress and economics, but above all it says that there is no limit to the endeavours of the human spirit. It is not, as is so often said, a poetry that confines or is confined; on the contrary, religious poetry owns the power to grasp the timeless out of the temporal. It sets up still, in a time of material prosperity (for some) a divine destiny for all men. It continues to urge that mankind may still rise above its own bathetic self. If the churches resist the changes going on around them, then the poet will stand outside such a church

It is easy to name poets who have so far enriched the life of poetry in English by creating a corpus of religious poetry: Donne, Herbert, Vaughan, Milton, Clare, Hopkins, Thomas, Daly, Hill ... and many more. Poetry that doesn't appear to make 'common sense', that may not shore up currently accepted notions and outlooks, is abandoned as irrelevant and an aberration; if the reading public expects humour, polemic, social comment, all of these are better catered for by other disciplines; religious poetry above all suffers from expectations! Good religious poetry is, simply, good poetry, with the added dimensions that

the untrammelled imagination brings to the work. Intellect is, of
course, involved in poetry, but there is more, and much more:
there is metaphor – (and here perhaps religious poetry delves
more deeply into metaphor) – there is emotion, feeling, music,
rhythm: and it is from an overall perspective here that 'poetry'
occurs. The reader, conditioned by so many things in our time, is
so easily closed off from participating in this experience by so
many false expectations. As Seamus Heaney comments in *The
Government of the Tongue:* 'The poet is credited with a power to
open unexpected and unedited communications between our
nature and the nature of the reality we inhabit'; for my purposes
here, 'unexpected' and 'unedited' are key words. One example,
merely. John Clare, 1793-1864, one of the strangest figures to
stomp through the landscape, was unlearned, was in love with a
woman whose death he refused to accept, spent years in an asylum, lost to reality, yet produced a volume of lyrical verse that
stood out strongly against the prevailing materialism of his
time; and it is in his poetry that there is a warming sense that he
knew himself pretty well and tried, despite his perceived crazi-
ness, to understand a world given to God's care. The religious
poetry he wrote saved him, and helps to save us, too:

> And he who studies nature's volume through
> And reads it with a pure unselfish mind
> Will find God's power all round in every view
> As one bright vision of the almighty mind
> His eyes are open though the world is blind
> No ill from him creation's works deform
> The high and lofty one is great and kind
> Evil may cause the blight and crushing storm
> His is the sunny glory and the calm.

Journey from Achill: The Atlantic God

An abiding memory of Achill Island: long before dawn, at the crossroads in Bunnacurry, family groups gathered to put an emigrant son or brother or father, sometimes even a daughter, on the early bus to Westport. From there a train would take them to Dublin, another train to the ferry port, and that was that; often for years; sometimes for ever. There were cases, trunks, bags and a restrained murmuring of voices. I do not remember any wailing, only that sense of a density of suffering consistent with helplessness, with the bleakness of rain, with the all-embracing demands of a faith that was negative in its impulses. I am speaking of Ireland, of the west of Ireland, of Achill, through the forties and fifties and even later. We cry, poor banished children of Eve, mourning and weeping, embracing our sufferings until we are spirited through to the great hereafter.

The Emigrants
I woke to a fraught and un-
familiar darkness; I sensed
the simperings of drifting rain,
pre-dawn breezes in the pines;

while I slept it had begun already,
the creaking of a cart,
the slow-rhythm, dull, steady
hoof-beats of a horse;

I dreamed through that comfortless noise.
And heard them then outside our gate,
the urgent, hushed, voices,
nervous shiftings against the dark;

a woman's call lifted high
in distress, like a furred animal
transfixed suddenly and I
was awake to the sound of the approaching

bus, its labouring through the gears to
stop. It stayed. Ticking.
I imagined the trunk, bulked and new,
tied round with fishing-rope,

how it was hoisted
up under tarpaulin on the bus roof;
then those awkward gestures and voices,
embarrassed kisses and knobbled words

like sand ramparts against a rising tide,
how the hurt was held back, the way
you hold your palm to your side
to contain the suffering. The bus

moved, loudly, labouring on the road
into silence. Silence. Then the creaking
of a cart, the same, slow rhythmic plod
of the hoof-beats of a horse.

It was always heart-breaking, but in those years the heart
broke silently; there was a great, an almost terrifying acceptance
that that was the way things were, and thank God that we had
our health, at least. The emigrants suffered their pains, their
loneliness, but they left at home those who perhaps suffered
more, who had to take all that suffering into their own hearts
and nurse it there, because God was good, and things were the
way they were.

Island Woman
It wasn't just the building of a bridge,
for even before they had gone by sea
to Westport, and from there abroad, and each

child sent money home till death in the family
brought him, reluctant, back. Of course the island
grew rich and hard, looked, they say, like Cleveland.

On a bridge the traffic moves both ways.
My own sons went and came, their sons, and theirs;
each time, in the empty dawn, I used to pray
and I still do, for mothers. I was there
when the last great eagle fell in a ditch.
My breasts are warts. I never crossed the bridge.

Our Roman Catholic faith was persistent as Achill rains, it
was associated then with physical and spiritual endurance, it
was vaunted as the force which maintained Ireland strong
down the centuries in spite of persecution, famine and deport-
ation. 'In spite of dungeon, fire and sword.' As a child I was
bathed in all of that, and the insidious power of aloofness and of
dogged determination held me back a little way from life.

Mother
God, on our island, insinuated himself –
like the thousand varieties of rain –
everywhere; soundless, shifting,

sometimes a brute and wailing
battering against our homes, a memory –
in our lives' dark outhouses –

of famine-gnawed, bitter people
herded onto piers.
Faith of our fathers, mother sang,

in spite of dungeon, fire and sword.

Her kingdom the resinous loft, school
girls about her, their hair, their smell,
how they huddled together derisively;

the priest, on the tiny altar,
took his cue from her,
breathless harmonium, diapason, celeste.

By the pamphlet rack,
by the window ledge,
where the unclaimed glove,

the beads, the sacred medal, lay with a few
dead and dying flies,
a darkwood staircase led

to mystical heights.

A vision before her of something perfect
she corrected us, ticking us off; be
true, she would say, be true to her

till death. She would sit with exercise books,
crossing the 't's, insistent, deft;
cancer spread in her and her body shrank,

blemishes, like ink-blots, on wrist and face;
her mind careened, ungovernable. She sat
high in her hospital bed, absorbed,

corrected hand-writing on her get-well cards.
When she died there were beads
under the pillow, a lip-stained cross,

the rosary bird, brooding.

Inevitably, in the mind of a child, the images and the thrust of such a faith run very deep. Yet I must always remind myself that all was by no means negative: the deeply universal beauty of much of the rituals and experiences of such an upbringing left a sense of holding to something true, mysterious and beautiful that could not be shaken off in a lifetime. There were the hymns, most of them bad but a few that touched on real music; there was the Latin, there was Bach and Vivaldi and Palestrina, there were the ritual movements, like a slow ballet, and so much more, in word and image that settled in the deepest recesses of the soul.

In Bunnacurry, Achill Island, there was a monastery of the Third Order of Saint Francis, established to counter the

Protestant 'colony' in Dugort that had appeared around famine times. The monastery had established a national school for boys and it was there I got my primary education. Thus, from the start, there was a 'militant' Catholic orientation in my life. We went to Mass in the monastery chapel, perhaps during the seasons of Lent and Advent, perhaps also on special feast days. I do remember that it was always early in the morning, and I drowsed; but I did experience, in that small chapel, a glow of a safe and warm surety, the brothers on their predieus beyond the rail that kept the tiny public back, their brown habits with the attractive cowl, the shuffling in the early morning light or dimness, the immediacy and accuracy of the Latin responses, the heads bowed for communion, the brother at the door smiling at us as we left, and I knew I would meet him again later on that day, in different circumstances. I have kept, and treasure, a shard of bright blue frosted glass from the door that led from the chapel down into the secret bowels of the monastery, a shard filled yet with memories, with goodness, service and with mystery.

The Monastery
On Achill Island it has been another tart summer;
the monastery gate has rusted closed
and monastery buildings crumble;

only the cemetery flourishes, Leo, Rufus, Anthony …
The chapel floor is rotting wood;
at dawn a pale blue ghost will cross

slowly, shivering. I keep a shard
of cobalt-blue glass upon a shelf,
savouring its light, its patterning.
*

With its sheds and orchards
an island upon an island;
I was white dough then in many hands;

we drove in the warmth of half sleep to Mass,
the slow, sedate black Anglia
parked on gravel where yellow light

reached from the chapel door;
we entered; in overhanging branches
rooks began to grumble.
*

Plaster saints
with plaster lilies in their hands
looked down on polished floors;

Angelo's head was straw;
his sandals slubbered on the chapel floor;
it was he who brought the candleflame

up from the cells to the honey, altar light;
the flame grew large and welcoming
behind the cobalt-blue glass of the door.

The brown coiffed figures on their predieus
were ranks of worker angels;
Angelo's head was straw; I heard him snore

and his head would loll
as if Botticelli's messenger forgot
for a moment, his awful declaration.
*

Brother Leo's one glass eye
could penetrate all wickedness
behind the lavatory walls;

his good eye watched you
watching the fixed stare of the other.
There were brass sliding trapdoors

over inkwells on the desks; 'dip' he would say
'your filthy fingernails down deep
and write the purity of God into your skulls'.

Those who forgot their Bible History
were made to chew on sour apples;
'the taste' he would say 'of sin is bitterness'.
*

Juniper's rhubarb pie
was two feet long, two inches wide;
"twon't take me long' he'd say 'to wait

a lifetime for my God'. Juniper
has been in the slaughter-house again, begging;
he will make such trotter soup,

such succulent stews that the poor
will rise from their beds and cry out to the Lord
oh Juniper, oh brother, Brother Juniper.

Juniper has cut
cloths from his cowl and habit;
he has shared out altar tapestries

and made vests for the labouring fishermen;
away on the road the tankers
ferry shark oil, shark blubber,

and the air thickens with the stench;
sometimes the hillside furze are molten gold
and rhododendron woods at Achill Sound

play hautboy processional music;
Juniper's pockets were deep, with traces of God
among mints, liquorice, and ticks of dust.

Even then – although this may be a willful interpretation
with the benefit of hindsight – I think I sensed some unease at
this faith. There were the people of Achill dressing up for
Sunday Mass, many of them standing about outside the church,
leaning against the wall, smoking, throwing eyes at the girls ...
until Mass was over, all of them seemingly given over to the
faith; and yet the whole panoply of Roman Catholicism seemed
to have nothing to do with their sufferings, the emigration, the

dole, their heaving of nets from curraghs, their scraping away at
sandy soil, their digging through the bogs for fuel. Only those
silly-seeming brothers who came out and walked and worked
among the people, appeared to me to have something more real
about them. And my love for Francis of Assisi must go very
much deeper than the magic of his myths, or the reality of his
presence among us even today.

To jump away a little, the sixties in Ireland stand out for me
as the end of the Middle Ages. As if suddenly, entirely new per-
spectives were opening up on every aspect of our living.
Challenges were put to every lane and alleyway of our faith and
for me the challenges proved too great: the faith had no response, I lost my faith. Perhaps my own awareness of the great
world outside the island of Achill, and outside the island of
Ireland, grew as the awareness of our century's woes began to
grow: Vietnam, the horrors of South Africa's apartheid system,
the struggles of the suffering poor in Latin America, the plight of
the very poor in Ireland as the thrust of our country and its public life moved towards glorifying the rich and the newly rich.
And everywhere I heard the answer of the church and it was
'No! No! No!' to any possibility of change and growth. Faith was
simply left behind; it was irrelevant; it even became an affront to
people trying to come to terms with the new Ireland.

Faith, in me, dwindled to a sentiment, an uneasiness; and yet
I continue to believe that there is more for mankind than this
mere trafficking in goods, in pleasure, in the lives of others less
well off. The sense of the need to search for real answers has
kept me restless. It was in reading Eberhard Bethge's life of
Dietrich Bonhoeffer that I began first to get a vague notion that
Christ ought to be brought in from the cold of Catholic dogma
and made to permeate the whole of everyday living. It was, if I
understand it rightly, a new 'worldly interpretation' of Christ
that could enrich our language and hence our lives. I dread the
jargon of politics, and of church politics in particular and I re-
sponded the more to Bonhoeffer with a sense of excitement, as
of something rich but undeveloped in the world I lived in.

Would it be, and is it still, a totally ludicrous hope that Christ-ness could pervade the language first and then the deeds of men-in-charge? Or will we see the untruth of political jargon lead ever and again towards holocaust?

In the Custody of the State
They came, those days, in Ford and Austin,
stood outside the chapel on the boundary wall;
words they used, gesticulating words;

sometimes the men threw hats into the air
that fell again, like shot pigeons.
They appeared, a while, on days

given over to the dead when we walked,
hands crossed awkwardly over the crotch,
the long walk to the yew field;

on Sundays, after prayers, we tensed
to the disembowelling of the hare and went home,
spent, after the masturbation. Bonhoeffer

had hoped that Christ the Leader
would conspire in the attempt on Hitler's life;
he heard someone crying loudly in the next cell,

words would not reach,
he banged on the wall between.
In Buchenwald, we were told,

a man held up his hands before his face,
saw them melt down to the bone in flames. But we,
they told us, knew enough of wars

never to be surprised again.
Today they come, in Saab and Peugeot,
cruise our streets with loud, recorded, words;

should you suggest – Christ –
as working hypothesis in Party, Senate, Dáil,
they will laugh, and cough, and sicken.

Bonhoeffer walked out calmly to the scaffold;
he climbed the wooden steps towards the omega;
brave and composed he stepped out onto darkness;

we go on crying against a great, blank wall.

From the encounter with Bonhoeffer it was an easy progres-
sion to the discovery of 'liberation theology'. I think the negative
response of Pope John Paul II to the liberation movement in
Nicaragua helped to focus my attention on what was happening
in Latin America. Leonardo Boff was also introduced into my
awareness by being summoned to explain himself before the
same gentleman. From Rome again it has been 'No! No! No!' (a
version of 'Out! Out! Out!' an attitude that has given another
word to our language, Thatcherism). But Boff's message, and
that of Gustavo Gutierrez, as well as the work of the great priest
and poet from Nicaragua, Ernesto Cardenal, excites me greatly,
and from it I see the hope for our world, and my personal path
towards understanding. (I think, too, this was the first time I associated poetry with what real religious living ought to be.)

This is talking 'revolution', but revolution in the sense of re-
volving, of going back yet again to the source, to the living,
working Jesus. It is talking 'revolution' in the sense of turning,
working, of changing one's ways; our 'cultural ethos is being in-
vaded destructively by the myth of progress in the capitalist
mould and its attendant focus on high consumption by small
elites' – Boff.

And it is talking 'revolution' in the sense that it seemed to
have been happening in East Germany, that we had hoped, for a
short and heart-warming summer, was happening in China,
bloodless, people-inspired, inevitable, and true.

In Achill Island there was a young man named Thomas
Patten, born 1910, who became unhappy with his people's lot
and worked to better it; this meant emigration to begin with, but
his heart was fired with the same love of the people that led so
many to Spain in 1936 to take up arms against that very fascism
that is more quietly rampant in our own times. His story tells of

revolution, of violent battle and its pointlessness, and the way
life goes on, the heavy, turning wheel of time. There is a stone
erected in Dooega, Achill, on which is written: 'Thomas Patten,
Achill, 1910-1936 who fought bravely and died in the defense of
Madrid, 1936, for the Spanish Republic and for all oppressed
people'.

Revolution
Born among these beautiful, tedious mountains,
these lazy-beds; names about him:
Inishgalloon, Gubglass, Loughanascaddy;

sea-kelp scattered on the fields;
beyond – the Atlantic, world movements;
night sky above the village
an armada of possibilities.

He would spread his rug out on Dooega Strand,
days when his father would still swim
and Grannie, leaning her back against the rocks,
loosened the blouse above her wholesome breasts;
he held the cranefly, daddy-long-legs, in his fist,
knew its scrabbling helplessness;

impatient he hurled rocks into the sea.

Kilburn, The Red Lion, where he paused
from his building of the city to be best man;
he wears a suit, a tie, a white carnation
and gazes out, with candour, on the future.

Then there were other names to deal with:
Guernica, Pamplona, Cordoba,
the dark bull of the people humbled in the ring
while the general, smiling, was having his portrait done;
death, the harvestman, tightening its limbs about him.

Dusk, Dooega Bay; a stone
set among heathers carries Patten's name;
he is watching out over the bay towards the stars;

a curragh has scraped home against the pier;
there are words, laughter, the echo of wood on wood;
to-morrow they will scatter dried sea-kelp over the fields.

The face of Thomas Patten gazing out from the stone over the ocean is a strong reminder of the ongoing suffering of the people, and of the indomitable will to better the people's lot. But in all of this our 'faith' still seemed irrelevant: until the realisation comes that the 'faith' we were hustled into is a divergence from the truth of Christ. The kingdom of God, as Boff points out, is already with us; its physical manifestation depends on the achievement of a total 'liberation' of all peoples from the shackles of poverty, exploitation, domination, and every move we make that enables this liberation to be developed more fully is a truly Christ-ian act. The most meaningful phrases I have encountered in decades come again from Leonardo Boff: 'The christic structure is anterior to the historical Jesus of Nazareth. It pre-exists within the history of humanity. Every time a human being opens to God and the other, wherever true love exists and egoism is surpassed, when human beings seek justice, reconciliation and forgiveness, there we have true Christianity and the christic structure emerges within human history ... With Jesus Christ, Christianity received its name. Jesus Christ lived it so profoundly and absolutely that his surname became Christ.' (from *Jesus Christ Liberator*, Leonardo Boff, SPCK 1980).

At last, in the writings and in the example of priests working in Latin America, I came to believe again in the possibility of a form of real Utopia. Here is an agenda, a Christian agenda, that gives thrust and meaning and hope to our activities. Francis of Assisi again becomes the great exemplar; or even someone as tortured and as true as Vincent Van Gogh; and suddenly, in a Dublin supermarket with its glut of supplies, I heard a call from far-away liberation theology:

Delikat-Essen
At the far right of the superstore
the meats garden – discreet lighting,
hallucinatory waterfalls;

only progressive democrats shop here,
feeding off lives
crushed under the belly of history;

neat rows of quail, all trussed and dainty
like young girls' breasts;
rabbits, hares, caught in flight and skinned,

laid out nude, purpling, like babies;
chops, here, have been dressed in frilly socks;
on trays, as if a Salomé had passed,

are livers, kidneys, hearts, and tongues.
Among these classically landscaped meatbeds –
low hedges of parsley sprigs,

cress, sculpted tomato busts –
you will find the names absent from history.
Oh to stand on a wooden Chiquita banana box

and urge theologies of liberation!
but all who come
nod to the government officials in their white coats,

machetes, bone-saws in their holsters,
and blood – like maps of Uruguay, Guatemala and Peru –
staining their elegant tuxedoes.

Against the awful and ongoing violence that seems endemic
to our times, liberation theology can set up an example of Christ-
ness. The awful tragedies brought about by the Bush regime in
America and the invasion of Iraq, the violence we have witnessed in the North of Ireland, the terrible beginnings to the
twenty-first century: all of that can be contained in the actuality
of one crime, as when a ransom note containing a severed finger

was placed behind the statue of St Thérèse of Lisieux, an unusually gruesome event touching one of the most gentle of our heroines:

Remembrance Day: Enniskillen
Behind the statue of St Teresa of the Flowers
a brown package, the message, the ransom note.
Somewhere a room where men in balaclavas

play at dice; safe houses. Rose petals
fall on us from the clouds. A soldier
broods over the named and the unnamed dead

of another war; the cenotaph; the empty tomb.
The gable end of a street
has swollen out like a balloon; our prayers

are pinned like poppies into our lapels.
Our arms have been growing into wreathes.
In the quiet of the night we go on crying, very hard.
*

After the bombardment apple-blossom fell
like snow in Normandy; retreating soldiers pushed
through Caen towards Paris. Under rubble of her town

a little saint lay undisturbed; I choose,
she had said, everything, her arms folded,
her eyes held down, turning and turning

in the chestnut-tree walk of her convent grounds,
the sky above her full of leaves, like prayers;
someone comes, with wheelbarrow and rake, and works

among the shadows of the trees. When they clothed her
snow fell on her garden, and the chestnut-trees
were apple orchards blossoming.

And Christ was on the Rood

The struggle to create a Christian world is an ongoing one, perhaps more difficult in our time than it has ever been, with the churches losing hold on the way people must live, the Vatican alienating itself from reality, the rise of Islam. The reality of our living is forever cruder than our dreams, the reality in the twenty-first century is so imperfect it is terrifying. We are overcome by acts of terror and the terror-acts that respond to them. Wars pile upon wars, each one more cruelly destructive than the one before. And we have grown aware of our changing universe, how nature continues on her own course of change by destruction, ably assisted by humanity's over-exploitation of the earth's resources. My concern has been how poetry has been able to face up to the reality and the dream.

In the late Middle Ages the clerical class was literate and the secular illiterate; this is not so any longer, indeed a hugely literate secular class has as good as dismissed the clerical and the latter has found no response but to thunder and repeat the old cries and exhortations. In the Middle Ages the Christian world was alert with penitential pilgrimages, associations for the service of the dead, indulgences and such like, most of it without any rational basis of truth. By the year 1500 official theory and actual popular belief had moved far apart from each other, as if the church was watching – and indeed had helped to urge – her congregations spin wildly out of her control. The use and abuse of images was widespread, the most common being, perhaps, that of St Christopher carried about to help avoid the dangers of dying. (Oh dear! And how many cars and trucks in our own time carry a smaller though similar image on their dashboards!) Icons and statues everywhere were the sources of miracles large and small, and the people, like all peoples stuck in doubt and darkness, longed for the reassurance of such exceptional events.

Henry VIII ordered daily Masses to be said for his soul for as
long as the world would last. The Black Death sent shock-waves
around the world. The people moved further away from strict
theological doctrines. Flagellants appeared and multiplied, hoping that in this way they might distance the miseries that came
thick and fast upon them. Miracle and passion plays gained
ground; they depended greatly on the grasping of the people's
minds by an immediate and striking imagery. In such a context
the great poem *The Dream of the Rood* appeared.

The Anglo-Saxon world seems to have remained simplistic
in its views of monsters, hell, and the tenets of the Christian religion. The language was still uninfluenced by the music of Latin
though it contained a vigour and immediacy that were rich in
their way. Peter Levi, in his introduction to *The Penguin Book of
English Christian Verse* (1984) remarks that 'there have been no
completely or thoroughly Christian centuries, and English has
never quite become a Christian language. Probably only the
dead Latin of the Middle Ages, a half-language, did that.' While
wondering exactly what he meant by English never quite becoming a Christian language, with R. S. Thomas and Geoffrey
Hill about, not to mention the earlier Herbert and Hopkins,
there is little doubt that English at every stage of its development has borne religious poetry very well indeed. Perhaps that
influence of Latin, when it passed through the mellifluous tones
of religious monastic singing, and through the musical and poetic
translations of the King James Bible, gave English a special
power. Narrow dogmatic rectitude that has dogged the clerical
embrace of religion in every age, never sits well with English; attempts by poets like John Skelton, even some of the didactic
efforts of George Herbert, read forced and leave the reader cold.
The very simplicity and urgency of the Anglo-Saxon language
helped lead more modern English into the religious sphere, with
some success. And perhaps it is that same rugged strength of
language won by Shakespeare and the poets of the seventeenth
century that makes religious poetry in the English language so
necessary for our own doubting and uncomforted souls.

When the dark swirling clouds of the strangeness of Anglo-Saxon literature began to clear for me, I found glimpses of strange worlds, worlds projected from the fears and longings, the harsh experiences of a primitive, suffering and besieged people. Dare I suggest that in our own time we have again approached that same condition? – of a primitive, suffering and besieged people! Heroes fought monsters. Great leaders were eulogised. It is easy to relish the Anglo-Saxon experience, *Beowulf, The Battle of Maldon, The Seafarer, The Wanderer*, as if the poems were not utterly relevant today. My belief is that they are still relevant, they retain their power to move, they issue from a world alert to its difficulties, they seek for hold and understanding, they touch on the transcendent.

The Dream of the Rood, which I studied in university, merely construing it with the same lip-in-teeth, puckered effort with which I had worked out Caesar's *Gallic Wars* for my secondary school exams, was the first actual poem that touched me, coming as I did from an island where the images of Christian striving, and particularly the crucifix, dominated every aspect of life. For some reason that short line that comes strategically, that sums up musically, rhythmically and thematically all that went before, all that is still to come, remained firmly in my memory and surfaced unbidden at strange moments: 'And Christ was on the Rood'. Christians have been 'glorying in the cross of Christ' for centuries; this poem, it could be argued, was the first to make the case for relics, for their preservation, veneration and storing in gilt caskets, the remains of a holy life! And yet the author of this piece was no simpleton, he knew the purpose and value of such items: 'that they make their prayers to me as a symbol', that honour should be given to the cross only in so far as it leads believers beyond itself and on to Christ. It could also be said that the poem was very much of its time, honouring the hero in battle, the basic image of Christ's ascent onto the cross one of a warrior willingly taking on the greatest danger in the service of others. Then, too, it partakes of and glorifies the tradition of presenting Christian teaching in dramatic form that was to issue in the great miracle and morality plays of those unlearned centuries.

I find the poem central to the fears and needs, indeed the whole seeking thrust, of our times. It is a poem that stands at the threshold of the great tradition of poetry, and of religious poetry, in the English language. I offer it in my own 'translation', and with it my translation of the great poem *The Seafarer*, in an effort to make them more accessible to our times, to contain with them that alliterative tread that carried them forward, and to present their undeniably literary power by bringing them forward into Dantesque lines.

The Dream of the Rood
(a version of the 7th/8th century Anglo-Saxon poem attributed to Cynewulf)
Pause with me while I tell the most precious, the best
of dreams, sent to me in the deep silence of night
when men, word mongers, were everywhere at rest.

It seemed that I saw the most marvellous tree
lifted high on the air, and all haloed in light,
most beautiful of all beams of wood; a beacon

bathed in gold; there were breathtaking gems that stood
all around the base, a further five were ablaze
high along the cross-beam. Holy angels of the Lord

looked always on its loveliness, enthralled.
This was no criminal's cross; there came to gaze
the saintliest of spirits, men everywhere and all

marvels of creation mused upon it where it stood.
How strange that tree of victory! and I – steeped in sin,
badly blemished all over – watched that glorious wood

adorned with banners, shining in all its beauty,
garlanded in gold, glorious gems worked in –
the wonderfully wreathed tree of the World's Ruler.

Yet straight through all that gold I could still see
the friend of once-wretched men, how it first began
to bleed on the right-hand side. Sorrow bore in on me,

and fear, before that vision; I saw the beacon change,
become clothed in colours; how at times the blood ran
drenching it in blood-dew, how it bloomed with a strange

beauty. I lay a long while, wretched at heart,
watching my Saviour's tree; until suddenly, most
wonderfully, the wood spoke, uttering these words:

'Long ago – distinctly I remember it! – one day
I was hewn down at the dark edge of the forest
and severed from my stem. Strong enemies seized me,

wrought me into a spectacle for the world to see,
commanding me to hoist their criminals on high;
men carried me on their shoulders and erected me

high on a hill – fixed there by many foes. I saw
the Ruler of mankind rush with real courage to climb
on me and I did not dare (my Lord had warned!)

bend down or break, though I saw the broad
surface of earth shiver. How simple – the Lord knows –
to smite His enemies! but firm and stout I stood,

unmoving. The hero stripped, though He was God Almighty!
robust and resolute, mounting onto the gallows
spirited, in the sight of many, to redeem mankind.

I wavered while the warrior embraced me: clasped me
and I did not dare bend down towards the ground,
fall on the earth's surface, I must stand fast.

I was raised up a Rood, carrying the powerful King,
high Lord of Heaven, and did not dare to bend.
They pierced me with bloody nails, the pain still stings!

the open wounds of malice; they made us fools
together. I was wholly wet with blood
streaming from His side when He gave up His soul

and helpless on that hill I knew a fearful fate:
stretched out in agony the Almighty God
of hosts cruelly wracked; the heavens all in spate

above the body of our Ruler, that bright radiance;
shadows reigned supreme under a thickening cloud;
all of creation mourned, moaned this cruel chance:

and Christ was on the rood.

'Now from afar came virtuous men, hastening
to that solitary Man. I saw it all, my many cares
grievously afflicting me, but I yielded to their chastening

humble and ardent hands. They held the God of Hosts,
took Him down from that dreadful torture; warriors
left me wet with moisture, wounded all over by arrows,

laid Him down, His limbs weary, stood watching at His head;
they looked on the Lord of heaven, resting for a time
weary from a woeful contest. A tomb was already made

in sight of those who slew Him, carved out of stone,
and they laid therein our Saviour, glorious, sublime.
They began to make their songs of sorrow, they mourned

until the fall of evening, then wearily wandered home
from that royal Throne, leaving Him there to rest.
We, however, a long while weeping, stood alone

on our foundations, fearing a dreadful destiny,
while that beautiful body chilled, that treasure chest
of life. Hastening then they hacked us cruelly

to the earth; planted us in a deep pit. Dark. Cold.
But the Lord's retainers, His friends, freed us, and then
set me on high, enhanced with silver and gold.

'Now, dear friend, now it is time that the world know
how I endured the wickedness of evil men
and grievous woes; it is time that the world show

honour to me through the whole earth and this broad
and marvellous creation; that they make their prayers
to me as a symbol. For on me did the Son of God

suffer agonies a while; so I won glory and was raised
high under the heavens, that I may heal the cares
of those who honour me and who offer praise.

Once, I became the most terrible of tortures, of pains
most odious to men, before I opened up for them,
for these word-mongers, life's true way.

See then how the prince of Heaven honoured me beyond
all the trees of the wood, true Keeper of the Kingdom,
as He honoured His mother Mary beyond all womankind.

'Now I require you, dear friend, that you relate
what you have seen to others, reveal in words this vision:
the tree of glory on which God himself had to tolerate

suffering for the ways of men and Adam's ancient sin,
that He tasted death; that He rose truly in great
honour to give help to men, mounted high to Heaven

and will come down on judgement day, angels at His side
to judge each man and woman in whatsoever way
they have measured out this transitory life. Nor let mankind

be unafraid of what the Ruler of the World will say!
Before the multitudes He will test, and try, to find
where is he who, for the Lord's sake, would taste

death's rancid savour as He did on the Rood!
They shall fear, for there are few who will discover
what to say to Christ that dreadfilled day. But you

who have borne on your breast this dear, divine
and best of symbols, have no fear, His blood
has won you grace over the gravity of earth for ever;

hope then always to dwell with Him in the highest Heaven.'

    Oh I prayed then with courage to that happy Cross,
I was alone, no person by, knew powerful longing. My food
now is to love that tree of victory, all else is loss

and forfeiture, to honour it more often than any man yet has.
My will is directed wonderfully towards the rood,
I have no powerful friends in the world, they have passed

from the dreams of earth to the King's glory and dwell
in Heaven now with the High Father. I long
for the day when the royal Rood of the Lord shall

fetch me finally from this transitory life and bring
me where is rapture and revelry in heaven, where all
the people of the Lord shall stand and sing

at the banquet where is bliss perpetual; and I pray
that our God who suffered on the gallows tree
be my friend, who has freed us to the light of day,

the Son and victor, stalwart, successful. He
who came with a glorious consort of spirits to stay
forever within God's kingdom; that I shall see

the Almighty Ruler, risen to where the angels stand,
with the holy company of saints at God's right hand,
the Hero, home with honour to His native land.

Seafarer
A reading of the Anglo-Saxon poem

(i)
May I relate a truthful tale from my life, tell
of a journey, how in long labour-filled days
I suffered whole hours of hardship, felt

bitter anguish, bore terrible anxieties,
was occupied so often in watches of the night
on a ship's prow in severe and pounding seas

when we tossed under cliffs and when my feet
were frozen and fettered with the chains
of frost. Cares festered in my heart and great

hunger came harrying my mind, oh I was a man
wearied by the sea. Still, how could you know –
or anyone who lives in luxury and ease on land –

how I, wretched and anxious, with the sea ice-cold,
must wander through winter on the exiles' trail,
far from my loving family, in misery untold,

icicles about me and showers of the sharpest hail,
the only sounds the sad echoing of brine
and the breaking surf. I'll have the swan's wail

for entertainment, the wearying gannet's whine,
curlews' calls in lieu of the laughter of men,
the seamew's cry in place of the pleasures of wine.

I remember tempests crashing on cliffs, the tern
was icy-feathered and often the eagle sang,
his feathers drenched with dew. None of my faithful kin

could comfort my soul in its distress. How wrong
it seems to you who live in the comfort of cities,
how little you know of journeys, terrifying, long;

when you're lazy, lusting from wine, how can you see
why I wearily pursue the ocean paths.

(ii)
                                                Out of the north
snow has fallen, frost is binding up the sea –

hail and freezing rain are falling on the earth.
Once more my courage fails as the thought forms
that I must venture out across the currents, go forth

on the commotion of salt waves. My soul warns
that I set out far from here and seek the homes
of people unknown to me. There is no one born –

no one so blessed with goods, no youth so callow,
so bold and brave in action, nor close to the heart
of his leader, but knows anxiety before a journey, knows

it is the Lord's demand determines he must go.

The pleasures of music and laughter, the love of his wife,
the comforts of this world: all are weariness to his mind,
nothing holds the seafarer save the harshness of his life,

the eagerness he knows for the ocean, to be far from land.
Woods may grow green and blossom, buildings seem fair,
heath and field are beautiful, nature hastening to expand –

all that but stirs the soul determined still and eager
to set out on the journey a spiritual life demands.

(iii)
The sad hail of the cuckoo, like a sacred harbinger,

stimulates the summer, the way seafaring sorrows
bring bitterness to the heart. How can the highborn know –
those couched in comfort – what certain men go through

who fare the farthest into areas of exile?
So now my own thoughts turn beyond known barriers,
wander widely out to the home of the huge whale,

to the very edge of earth, and longing leaves me
eager and hungry, the calls of the lonely bird
urge me irresistibly out on the way of the sea

because the joys of the service and love of the Lord
are dearer far to me than this dead life,
time transitory here on earth as any trysting word.

Earthly goods will not stand a man eternally; always
something takes him at the appointed time: disease
or age or violence will carry him away;

so, in proud assemblies nothing can equal praise
from the living, for those lordly men who have achieved,
before their death, their due of good works, whose days

passed magnanimously on earth, in spite of the malice
of enemies, whose bravery faced with evil is well known
and brings honourable mention to men's lips. And this

praise lives afterwards among the angels, in the glory
of eternal life, with hymns of joy among angelic hosts
for ever.

(iv)
                    Ages pass, so too the pomp and store

of earthly riches, no king, no emperor remains,
no generous patrons; each person must achieve
his own great and glorious deeds, must strive alone

for honour; gone are worldly joys, those hosts are gone,
the morally weak are with us still, living in the ease
of their feeble labours. Honour, integrity, have flown,

for the true grow wizened and wither as any on the face
of the earth, features grow pale, and the fever
of grief comes with grey hairs, with memories of great

and valued friends who have left the earth forever.
The flesh grows flaccid as life's tide ebbs away,
sweet things don't suit the palate, all tastes bitter,

see how hands stiffen, how thoughts go suddenly astray.
Though you build monuments of gold to his memory
your brother still must lie amongst the dead, and why

bury with him the treasures his busyness achieved,
what use such tatters and trinkets to a soul in sin,
what consolation, before God's terror, can gold be,

pitifully piled away during a life's long attrition?
The earth itself will crumble at the Creator's word,
who fixed the universe on immovable foundations,

who shaped the firmament, the sea, the whole world.
He is foolish who does not fear the Lord; death, too soon,
will fall on him. He who lives a humble life and good

is blessed; these favours fall on him from Heaven, too,
with grace and faith and all that's good, from God.
A man's mind must steer him strongly and stay true

to promises, he must fare honestly. And every man
must know moderation, avoid evil, always strive
to keep his will fixed firm as a rudder against sin.

Let us think then where our true home lies
and learn how we may sail thereto, and learn to win
God's grace against the fateful meeting where man's life

will be blessed by the Lord's love in the port of heaven,
by Him who has honoured us though we sin and sin again,
the Prince of Glory, the great Captain for ever. Amen.

Woefully Arrayed:

John Skelton, skittering towards religious verse

John Skelton is one of those shadowy figures in the early growth of English literature about whom very little is known. He appears as a lively and somewhat naughty man, hopping across the fens and marshlands of an England not yet disrupted by religious controversy. Chaucer had already stalked out of darkness into a dim forge where he had begun to beat the language into exciting shape. Now that forge was almost empty once again and Shakespeare had not yet become a grin on his father's scarce-bearded face. In the voice of a nun lamenting her dead bird, Skelton writes:

> But for I am a maid,
> Timorous, half afraid,
> That never yet assay'd
> Of Helicon's well,
> Where the Muses dwell;
> Though I can read and spell,
> Recount, report, and tell
> Of the Tales of Canterbury,
> Some sad stories, some merry ...

He goes on to refer to the story of Gawain, and of Arthur's 'knights commendable' and, still suggesting the nun's simplicity, perhaps wishing to show his own broad learning, he lists an impressive lot of classical authors and mythic yarns:

> Gower's English is old,
> And of no value told;
> His matter is worth gold,
> And worthy to be enrolled ...
> Also John Lydgate
> Writeth after a higher rate ...

Born in the early 1460s, John Skelton may have originated somewhere in Yorkshire. He was educated in the Universities of Cambridge and Oxford and won a higher degree in rhetoric in 1488. He received further recognition from the University of Louvain in 1492. He acquired a reputation as a rhetorician and a translator and joined the service of Henry VII. The first work we know that is surely his, *Elegy on the Death of the Earl of Northumberland*, was published in 1489. He was also working on the translation of Diodorus Siculus when he was made tutor to Prince Henry who was to become King Henry VIII. He later wrote and published books on pedagogy.

Skelton's early skirmishes with writing were, then, typical of that time: secular, learned, rhetorical, much of it bent towards gaining advancement in courtly circles. But in 1498 he was ordained priest of the Abbey of St Mary Grace and in that year wrote a book of satire on court politics. Some sort of disillusionment had set in. Shortly after that he was involved in a court dispute which put him into prison for a short while over an unpaid debt. The signs appeared clear: get out, fast; *hie thee to a monastery*, win quiet and write in peace.

He retired about 1503 and became rector of the parish church in Diss, Norfolk, as a reward for his years of service. Around 1505, Skelton wrote *Phyllyp Sparrowe*, perhaps his most famous work, the lament of a young nun for her pet bird. The poem is lively, funny, and beautifully carried forward. In 1512 he published an elegy in Latin for Henry VII at the request of the abbot of Westminster. All of this seems to have gained him favour once again and by 1512 he was back in court, finding retirement too dull for him, or his prospects brighter. He was given the title of King's Orator by Henry VIII. In the following years he wrote poems on the defeat of the French, the Scots, and James IV. Things were going well; he moved to a house in the sanctuary of Westminster in 1518 and shortly thereafter began his attacks on Cardinal Wolsey, works like *Speak, Parrot, Colin Cloute* and *Why Come Ye Not to Court?* (1522). His attacks on Wolsey were aimed, perhaps, at getting him further favour in the eyes of Henry VIII, lauding Henry over Wolsey and suggesting various nefarious schemes of the Cardinal's. The vitriol and satire are often really intense:

> So mani vagabonds, so mani beggars bold,
> So much decai of monasteries and religious places;
> So hot hatred against the Church, and chariti so cold;
> So much of 'my lord's grace', and in him no grace is ...
> So far a maggot, bred of a flesh-fly;
> Was never such a filthi gorgon, nor such an epicure.

This from *Speak, Parrot*. And much more in like vein. He goes on in a later poem, *Colin Cloute*, to emphasise his satire, this time greatly against the clergy in general, and the Cardinal in particular:

> How ye break the dead's wills,
> Turn monasteries into water-mills,
> Of an abbey ye make a grange;
> Your works, they say, are strange;
> So that their founders' souls
> Have lost their bead-rolls,
> The money for their masses
> Spent among wanton lasses.

There is a sense of genuinely-felt anger in these poems, anger against hypocrisy and injustice but there is also the sense that he is still courting Henry's favour. It is interesting to note how Skelton writes best out of an assumed *persona*, the nun in *Phillip Sparrow*, the parrot, and here as Colin Cloute, a rustic (though learned) gentleman who, while dressed in rags and speaking from a poor man's perspective, exhibits learning and wit beyond the norm. Rhyme, too, is both Skelton's strength and weakness; few have continued a rhyme for as many lines as he, yet there are times when the rhymes take over and lead him by the nose.

He pushed Wolsey to the extreme in these poems and yet, as soon as he grew aware that Wolsey held and increased Henry's favour, and that his own poetic outpourings were not drawing

Henry's smiles on himself, Skelton abruptly changed tack and wrote new and laudatory poems dedicated to Wolsey. This does not take from the earlier work; indeed, it was a time when the courting of the King's blessings in any way possible was an accepted and indeed essential mode of behaviour. Skelton's apologetic and autobiographical *The Garland of Laurel* (1523) appeared after he had made his peace with Wolsey. Skelton died peacefully on 21 June 1529, the day that Catherine of Aragon pleaded before King Henry VIII. The tradition that he died in sanctuary at Westminster cannot be proved.

Skelton stands on the patio step between the Middle Ages and the English renaissance. The great creative impulse of the Middle Ages was ebbing, the English Renaissance had not yet struggled to its birth. He is one of the earliest poets whose success touches on the development of the language. He is also one of the very first poets in which the impulse to write religious verse strikes home, the first individual voice and name that we have in this area. *The Dream of the Rood*, a poem Skelton must have known, takes the voice of the cross, and speaks out of that *persona*. Remembering Skelton's penchant for the *persona* approach to poetry, one can feel that influence shadowing Skelton's religious work.

His language was very much in touch with the common speech of the day and many of his rhymes and songs were widely known and performed at wild gatherings. His life, that mixture of court politics, private concerns and priestly duties, seems typical of the age. He appears to have misbehaved and repented, in most of the positions he occupied. Erasmus called him 'the one light and glory of British letters', mainly because of his expertise in the translation of Latin works. There are tales about Skelton that rival those of Rabelais, and his later hectoring and satirical angers made him both feared and detested. As he was growing old he regarded himself as 'the British Catullus' and on his deathbed is known to have confessed to a marriage and several children. His poetry did, indeed, draw on the demotic though his sacred verse remains firmly in the 'high style'.

The poem already mentioned, *Philip Sparrow*, written in quick-moving, heavily-rhyming short lines, begins as a mock elegy on the death of a pet sparrow belonging to a young nun. In many ways it anticipates the mock-heroic works of Pope and Dryden, the fun, the linguistic playfulness in rhyme and suggestive association. There is a clever interlacing of lines and phrases from the Latin Mass for the Dead. This is Skelton at his most lovable and roguish, enjoying his learning, relishing language.

> For, as I before have said,
> I am but a young maid,
> And cannot in effect
> My style as yet direct
> With English words elect:
> Our natural tongue is rude,
> And hard to be ennewed
> With polished terms lusty;
> Our language is so rusty,
> So cankered, and so full
> Of frowards, and so dull,
> That if I would apply
> To write ornately,
> I wot not where to find
> Terms to serve my mind.

It is, however, as one of the first of the poets who touched on religious themes, that he interests me. His originality in religion is slight, his verses predictable, but *Woefully Arrayed* rings true and offers a genuine personal pleading, as if these are the words of one aware of the darkness of his own nature. This popular poem rings with echoes of *The Dream of the Rood* and with a sense of form that anticipates the personal call and mastery of George Herbert. There is a link, too, between the medieval traditions of morality and miracle plays, and a more modern personal approach to religion and poetry. It is good to see the fading away of allegory throughout his work.

Here is one of his other poems:

Prayer to the Father of Heaven

O Radiant Luminary of light interminable,
Celestial Father, potential God of might,
Of heaven and earth O Lord incomparable,
Of all perfections the Essential most perfite!

O Maker of mankind, that formed day and night,
Whose power imperial comprehendeth every place!
Mine heart, my mind, my thought, my whole delight
Is, after this life, to see thy glorious Face.

Whose magnificence is incomprehensible,
All arguments of reason which far doth exceed,
Whose Deity doubtless is indivisible,
From whom all goodness and virtue doth proceed,

Of thy support all creatures have need:
Assist me, good Lord, and grant me of thy grace
To live to thy pleasure in word, thought, and deed,
And, after this life, to see thy glorious Face.

It is tempting to see the priest in his pulpit declaiming this piece to a stunned congregation. It is also tempting to see it flung against the wily Wolsey as an example of Skelton's mastery in learning and didacticism. A finely versed poem, moving with an ease of metre and rhyme that is intended to be, and is, seductive. Yet that Father outlined in the Latinate language of the first stanza and the first half of the second, is surely a Being utterly and forever remote from the prayerful individual. The poem does not really touch us until the grandiose language fades into the simple statement, 'of thy support all creatures have need'; from there on the lines have a simplicity and personal honesty about them that leave a sense of true prayer in the mind of the reader; now it is 'good Lord', and a direct plea for aid. The Father of light interminable has become a grace-giving God, and the last line is more a genuine plea where the last line of the first stanza is read as if provoked by priestly duty.

To The Second Person
O benign Jesu, my sovereign Lord and King,
The only Son of God by filiation,
The Second Person withouten beginning,
Both God and man, our faith maketh plain relation,
Mary thy mother, by way of incarnation,
Whose glorious passion our soules doth revive,
Against all bodily and ghostly tribulation
Defend me with thy piteous woundes five.

O peerless Prince, painéd to the death
Ruefully rent, thy body wan and blo, *(livid)*
For my redemption gave up thy vital breath,
Was never sorrow like to thy deadly woe!
Grant me, out of this world when I shall go,
Thine endless mercy for my preservative:
Against the world, the flesh, the devil also,
Defend me with thy piteous woundes five.

Although these poems go somewhat automatically through
the forms offered about faith in the Trinity, and although the
heavy words continue – filiation, tribulation, preservative – yet
there is a closeness to the subject that guarantees its authenticity;
phrases like 'ruefully rent, thy body wan and blo', 'vital breath';
even words like 'sorrow' and 'revive' and 'defend' are simple
and immediate and allow for an effective and somewhat moving poem. It must be remembered always that with John Skelton
we are only beginning to stir out of the dark wood and into the
vast and sunlit plain of English language poetry and of personal
belief expressed in poetry.

When we come to the great poem 'Woefully Arrayed', we
seem to step out into another landscape. There is controversy
surrounding the authorship of the poem but the arguments and
concerns here are deeply academic and do not affect the worth
of the piece. In the careful shaping and rhyming of the poem, in
its clear musicality and repetitions, in its language hovering between a more modern English and a Chaucerian one, in its hark-

ing back to the dream form of *The Dream of the Rood* and the placing of the work in the mouth of someone other than the author,
in this case, Christ, there is the touch of John Skelton. The dramatic stance is reminiscent of the morality and miracle plays,
and indeed the other poems manifest the same desire to teach, to
preach, to instruct the unlearned. Yet the development from the
intellectual approach of the poems above, to this pathos and
emotional closeness, is quite startling. Leave the 'argumentify-
ing' to the academics; the poem stands, a glory in itself, the first
truly magnificent expression in English verse, of a religious sensibility expressing itself wholly through poetry.

> *Woefully Arrayed*
> Woefully arrayed,
> My blood, man,
> For thee ran,
> It may not be nay'd;
> My body blue and wan,
> Woefully arrayed.
>
> Behold me, I pray thee, with thy whole reason,
> And be not so hard-hearted, and for this encheason, *(reason)*
> Sith I for thy soul sake was slain in good season,
> Beguiled and betrayed by Judas' false treason:
>   Unkindly entreated,
>   With sharp cord sore fretted,
>   The Jewés me threated:
> They mowéd, they grinned, they scornéd me, *(mouthed)*
> Condemnéd me to death, as thou may'st see,
>   Woefully arrayed.
>
> Thus naked am I nailed, O man, for thy sake!
> I love thee, then love me; why sleepest thou? awake!
> Remember my tender heart-root for thee brake,
> With painés my veinés constrained to crake: *(crack)*
>   Thus tuggéd to and fro,
>   Thus wrappéd all in woe,
>   Whereas never man was so,

Entreated thus in most cruel wise,
Was like a lamb offered in sacrifice,
    Woefully arrayed.

Of sharp thorn I have worn a crown on my head,
So painéd, so strainéd, so ruefull, so read,
Thus bobbéd, thus robbéd, thus for thy love dead, *(beaten)*
Unfeignéd I deignéd my blood for to shed:
    My feet and handés sore
    The sturdy nailés bore:
    What might I suffer more
Than I have done, O man, for thee?
Come when thou list, welcome to me,
    Woefully arrayed.

Of record thy good Lord I have been and shall be:
I am thine, thou art mine, my brother I call thee.
Thee love I entirely – see what is befall'n me!
Sore beating, sore threating, to make thee, man, all free:
    Why art thou unkind?
    Why hast not me in mind?
    Come yet and thou shalt find
Mine endless mercie and grace –
See how a spear my heart did race, *(wound)*
    Woefully arrayed.
Dear brother, no other thing I of thee desire
But give me thine heart free to reward mine hire:
I wrought thee, I bought thee from eternal fire:
I pray thee array thee toward my high empire
    Above the orient,
    Whereof I am regent,
    Lord God omnipotent,
With me to reign in endless wealth:
Remember, man, thy soul's health.

Woefully arrayed,
My blood, man,
For thee ran,
It may not be nay'd;
My body blue and wan,
Woefully arrayed.

There is that personal touch, new and fresh and moving, 'I love thee, then love me'; here already is George Herbert; this, in the context of the drama of the poem, is a teacher's exquisite point, a Skelton move, a preacher's trick. Yet its very immediacy and simplicity give it honour and truth. In the rhyming power, in the swift onward movement of the verse, here is Hopkins already. In the deep sorrow and genuine urgings of the poem, R. S. Thomas can already be heard. With John Skelton, if in fact he did write this poem, the dark door out of the forge has begun to open.

The Passionate Man's Pilgrimage

Walter Raleigh, 1554-1618, soldier, adventurer and lover, was active in Ireland and helped to suppress Irish resistance. He was made a knight by Elizabeth in 1584 and Captain of the Guard in 1587. Perhaps the greatest force in Raleigh's life was the one that urged him to climb the social and court ladders, and indeed the central 'love' of his life was the love he protested to his queen, yet the two poems attributed to him show (as did his real marriage and real family affections) that a religious awareness was never far from his mind during his adventurous and turbulent life. It may well be the inconstancies of court life that urged him towards the constancy of his God and it was the prospect of a violent end forever looming over him that made him aware of the futility of all that he was greedily seeking in life. He married secretly the queen's maid of honour and she never truly forgave him; he fell from favour, was imprisoned, and later released to carry out explorations on Elizabeth's behalf. James I had him imprisoned again and eventually beheaded. On the scaffold he spoke of his love of God. It is believed that *The Passionate Man's Pilgrimage* was actually written while he was waiting for the scaffold, though this may be little more than a pleasing fancy. The poem brings memories of *The Seafarer*, the idea of life as a pilgrimage through rough ways to one's God, and pilgrimage was a very potent image right through the Middle Ages and even into our own era.

> Give me my scallop-shell of quiet,
> My staff of faith to walk upon,
> My scrip of joy, immortal diet,
> My bottle of salvation,
> My gown of glory, hope's true gage,
> And thus I'll make my pilgrimage.

Blood must be my body's balmer,
No other balm will there be given,
Whilst my soul like a white palmer
Travels to the land of heaven,
Over the silver mountains,
Where spring the nectar fountains;
And there I'll kiss
The bowl of bliss,
And drink my eternal fill
On every milken hill.
My Soul will be a-dry before,
But after it will ne'er thirst more.

And by the happy blissful way
More peaceful pilgrims I shall see,
That have shook off their gowns of clay
And go apparelled fresh like me.
I'll bring them first
To slake their thirst,
And then to taste those nectar suckets
At the clear wells
Where sweetness dwells,
Drawn up by saints in crystal buckets.

And when our bottles and all we
Are filled with immortality,
Then the holy paths we'll travel,
Strewed with rubies thick as gravel,
Ceilings of diamonds, sapphire floors,
High walls of coral and pearl bowers.

From thence to heaven's bribeless hall
Where no corrupted voices brawl,
No conscience molten into gold,
Nor forged accusers bought and sold,
No cause deferred, nor vain-spent journey,
For there Christ is the King's Attorney,
Who pleads for all without degrees,
And he hath angels, but no fees.

When the grand twelve million jury
Of our sins with sinful fury
'Gainst our souls black verdicts give,
Christ pleads his death, and then we live.
Be thou my speaker, taintless pleader,
Unblotted lawyer, true proceeder;
Thou mov'st salvation even for alms,
Not with a bribed lawyer's palms.

And this is my eternal plea
To him that made heaven, earth and sea;
Seeing my flesh must die so soon,
And want a head to dine next noon,
Just at the stroke when my veins start and spread,
Set on my soul an everlasting head.
Then am I ready, like a palmer fit,
To tread those blest paths which before I writ.

Who Lord? Me?

The Fletcher Brothers

1587, execution of Mary Queen of Scots. 1603 James I comes to the throne and in 1604 bans the Jesuits from the country. 1605 The Gunpowder Plot; Guy Fawkes and other Roman Catholic conspirators fail in an attempt to blow up Parliament and James I; focus of hatred turns firmly towards Roman Catholicism. 1611, James I's authorized version (King James Version) of the Bible is completed; and in 1620 Pilgrims land at Plymouth Rock on Cape Cod, Massachusetts, in the *Mayflower*.

And so the end of the sixteenth and the start of the seventeenth centuries in England were times of strife and self-examination. Religious struggles had already brought martyrs on every side, and would bring more. Queen Elizabeth had brought some steadiness and political surety for a time, and her reign settled the Anglican Church into power and authority. But everyone was aware that there existed a large number of people who still held with Rome, and gradually the reasons why England had broken with papal authority slipped into the background of consciousness. The Puritans left for fresher pastures where they might live their intense faith more securely. Sermonising grew in importance and sermons grew in length. A family appeared, the Fletchers, who were Anglican from the topmost hairs of their heads to their toe-nails. And they wished to pass on their faith in sermon and poem. A little like John Donne, a little like Gerard Manley Hopkins many years later, the sermons were somewhat baked with a tasking, long-winded and learned flour; many of the poems suffered from the same wet dough, but here and there a poem came from the mix and offered real nourishment. And one of the Fletcher poems strikes me as unjustly ignored in the long line of religious poetry in English.

Giles Fletcher senior was of a family that included the Bishop of London and a dramatist, John Fletcher. The latter is well known for his collaboration with Francis Beaumont and even with Shakespeare. Phineas and Giles were sons of Giles senior who was an MP, and had a career in the public service until 1611 when he died, aged 72. He was highly respected as a public figure and in 1593 he published *Licia*, in his retirement, a cycle of love-sonnets. At this time there was an emphasis on the Italian sonnet form, and Giles senior executed his own sonnets with some skill. His two sons were brought up by a man eager and proficient in poetry.

Phineas Fletcher was born in 1582, his brother Giles was born in 1586, in Kent. In 1600 Phineas entered Kings College Cambridge and graduated with an MA in 1608. Phineas was ordained and became chaplain to Sir Henry Willoughby who gave him a rectory in Norfolk. Here he married and lived out the rest of his days. He attacked the Jesuits in several poems and pamphlets and was very much aware of the antagonisms in religion around this time. He also wrote plays and theological treatises. In 1633 his most important work appeared, *The Purple Island*, a collection of long and miscellaneous poems. *The Purple Island* itself is a long poem, allegorically describing the structure of the human body and mind. He portrays the veins as rivers, the bones as mountains, the brain is personified. The poem is remembered today more for its fine landscape pictures. Also called *The Isle of Man, The Purple Island* is a mixed blessing of a poem! Here are some of the early stanzas that are descriptive and pleasant:

Happy, thrice happy times in silver age!
When generous plants advanc't their lofty crest;
When honour stoopt to learn'd wisdomes page;
When baser weeds starv'd in their frozen nest;
    When th' highest flying Muse still highest climbes;
    And virtues rise keeps down all rising crimes.
Happy, thrice happy age! happy, thrice happy times!
(…)

Oft therefore have I chid my tender Muse;
Oft my chill breast beats off her fluttering wing:
Yet when new spring her gentle rayes infuse,
All storms are laid, I 'gin to chirp and sing:
    At length soft fires disperst in every vein,
    Yeeld open passage to the thronging train,
And swelling numbers tide rolls like the surging main.

It goes on, however, and describes the island of the body, a
dangerous task and one that leads to such stanzas as the following:

The whole Isle, parted in three regiments,
By three Metropolies is jointly sway'd;
Ord'ring in peace and warre their governments
With loving concord, and with mutuall aid:
    The lowest hath the worst, but largest See;
    The middle lesse, of greater dignitie:
The highest least, but holds the greatest soveraigntie.

Down in a vale, where these two parted walls
Differ from each with wide distending space,
Into a lake the Urine-river falls,
Which at the Nephros hill beginnes his race:
    Crooking his banks he often runs astray,
    Lest his ill streams might backward finde a way:
Thereto, some say, was built a curious framed bay.

A brave attempt but a poem mostly now unreadable. In it can
be seen the urge of the time and of the parson to teach and instruct, to give sermons in whatever form may capture the mind
of the reader or listener. And this, too, was the urge of his
younger brother, Giles.

Giles Fletcher junior took a degree from Cambridge in 1606.
He wrote a poem on the death of Queen Elizabeth but is mainly
known for his work *Christ's Victory*. He was ordained priest and
became famous as a sermoniser. He was given the rectory of
Alderton in Suffolk, but found his parishioners so unresponsive
that he appears to have lost heart in ministry and, indeed, in life.

He died in 1623, aged only 37. His poem *Christ's Victory and Triumph, in Heaven, in Earth, over and after Death,* is epic in scope, its stanza form reminiscent of Spenser's and parts of the poem are known to have appealed to Milton. Here, too, there is a pleasing sense of nature, though vague and distant, but most of all there is the urge to show, to tell, to preach, so that the poem yet feels as if it were taking the reader by the lapels and murmuring into the ear a distinct message. The mind of the writer is in it, and his faith, his heart, too, but not his person!

There might the violet, and primrose sweet
> Beams of more lively, and more lovely grace,
> Arising from their beds of incense meet;
> There should the swallow see new life embrace
> Dead ashes, and the grave unheal his face,
> To let the living from his bowels creep,
> Unable longer his own dead to keep:
There heav'n and earth should see their Lord awake from
> sleep.

Their Lord, before by other judg'd to die,
> Now Judge of all himself; before forsaken
> Of all the world, that from his aid did fly,
> Now by the Saints into their armies taken;
> Before for an unworthy man mistaken,
> Now worthy to be God confess'd; before
> With blasphemies by all the basest tore,
Now worshipped by Angels, that him low adore.

Whose garment was before indipt in blood,
> But now, imbrighten'd into heav'nly flame,
> The Sun itself outglitters, though he should
> Climb to the top of the celestial frame,
> And force the stars go hide themselves for shame:
> Before that under earth was buried,
> But now about the heavens is carried,
And there for ever by the Angels heried.

It was an age of sermonisers, an age when the great miracle

and morality plays were long vanished, an age of sophistication
where such playthings would appear unworthy. It was an age of
high seriousness, and yet there is one poem that stands out from
the Fletcher gatherings, a poem written by Phineas Fletcher and
called *The Divine Lover*. It is different from the other works because it has the urgency of the personal within it, a personal response echoing that of John Donne and equaling some of the
poems of George Herbert. It is, I feel, a poem that deserves to be
cherished out of all the cartloads of works the Fletcher family
came up with.

> *The Divine Lover*
>   Me, Lord? Canst thou mispend
>   One word, misplace one look on me?
>   Call'st me thy Love, thy Friend?
>   Can this poor soul the object be
> Of these love-glances, those life-kindling eyes?
> What? I the centre of thy arms' embraces?
>   Of all thy labour I the prize?
>   *Love never mocks, Truth never lies.*
> Oh how I quake: Hope fear, fear hope displaces:
> I would, but cannot hope: such wondrous love amazes.
>
>   See, I am black as night,
>   See, I am darkness: dark as hell.
>   Lord, thou more fair than light;
>   Heaven's sun thy shadow: can suns dwell
> With shades? 'twixt light and darkness what commerce?
> *True: thou art darkness, I thy Light: my ray*
>   *Thy mists and hellish fogs shall pierce.*
>   *With me, black soul, with me converse;*
> *I make the foul December flowery May.*
> *Turn thou thy night to me: I'll turn thy night to day.*
>
>   See, Lord, see, I am dead:
>   Tombed in myself: myself my grave.
>   A drudge: so born, so bred:
>   Myself even to myself a slave.

Thou Freedom, Life: can Life and Liberty
Love bondage, death? *Thy Freedom I: I tied*
  To loose thy bonds: be bound to me:
  My yoke shall ease, my bonds shall free.
Dead soul, thy Spring of life, my dying side:
There die with me to live: to live in thee I died.

That beginning: 'Me, Lord?' and 'can You call me Friend?'
This is pure George Herbert, as is the dialogue form between
sinner and Lord, the protest, the answering reasoning, the
pleading, the rhyme, the form, though Herbert's poem is more
compact, more terse and more dramatic, and is based on a richer
sense of thought that Fletcher's. Even the titles echo each other,
The Divine Lover and *Love*. I believe Herbert must have known
this poem and, consciously or unconsciously, made use of it. It is
just a pity Herbert's greater poem has hidden this one from our
gaze. In itself it is vigorous, surging forward, deeply felt and
rich with the wit and anomalies that John Donne gloried in. And
it, too, is written in the form of a sermon to himself, an admoni-
tion, and develops towards a climax of faith and hope, as does
Herbert's poem.

The Burning Babe

Robert Southwell (1561-1595)

Robert Southwell lived and died in very troubled times, times that touched all he did and thought and wrote. He was born in Norfolk and went abroad in 1576 to study at Douai. There he was inspired by the Jesuits and entered that order. He was ordained priest in 1584 and returned to the highly dangerous English Mission at his own request. There are those for whom religion is a dangerous obsession, there are others whose obsession with danger is a religious thing! He came to England in 1586 and worked for some years, evading arrest. His missionary work was zealous and he found refuge moving between Catholic houses. Safe houses! He was generally seen as a gentle, unpolitical soul, staying at a distance from religious disputes. But he was taken in 1592, examined many times, suffered prolonged torture on the rack and otherwise and was eventually beheaded at Tyburn.

For Southwell, naturally enough, life is exile; the poems were written during his time in England and were intended to convince Catholics that their case was like that of the early Christians and worth their efforts to stand firm. His poems also offered a preference for death. By his training he was already aware of the power of words and the possibilities of eloquence; this latter penchant mars some of his preaching poems. He has a strong delight in paradox, in this way anticipating the 'metaphysical' poets and Donne may well have picked up some of this from him. He is interesting in that, in lines like 'All wealth is want where chiefest wishes fail – / Yea, life is loathed, where love may not prevail', there is a moment hovering between the Anglo-Saxon and the Renaissance. And surely there is a forethought of Donne in 'I live, but such a life as ever dies; I die, but such a death as never ends; My death, to end my dying, life de-nies, And life, my living death no whit amends'. And it may not be too much to see Hopkins reading a fellow-Jesuit poet, a fellow-sufferer, in later years and relishing this love for words and their emotional resonances.

The Burning Babe
As I in hoary Winter's night stood shivering in the snow,
Surpris'd I was with sudden heat, which made my heart to
      glow;
And lifting up a fearful eye, to view what fire was near,
A pretty Babe all burning bright did in the air appear;
Who scorched with excessive heat, such floods of tears did
      shed,
As though his floods should quench his flames, which with
      his tears were bred:
Alas (quoth he) but newly born, in fiery heats I fry,
Yet none approach to warm their hearts or feel my fire, but I;
My faultless breast the furnace is, the fuel wounding thorns:
Love is the fire, and sighs the smoke, the ashes, shames and
      scorns;
The fuel Justice layeth on, and Mercy blows the coals,
The metal in this furnace wrought, are men's defiled souls:
For which, as now on fire I am to work them to their good,
So will I melt into a bath, to wash them in my blood.
With this he vanished out of sight, and swiftly shrunk away,
And straight I called unto mind, that it was Christmas day.

East or West?

A Good Friday Meditation

It may be salutary every now and again to remind ourselves of the possible inherent value of suffering. Ireland has long been fiddling about at a crossroads; the largest and most glaring sign points west: to prosperity, self-aggrandisement, wealth and power. The lesser one, grimy from years of neglect and dust, points east: not back to where we have come from, but towards a new perspective on faith, charity and hope. Decisions, decisions! West, towards the glory and ease of a wonderfully setting sun (it is setting, however); or East, towards the demands of a chilly and rising sun (to be followed by a day of difficult labour); West, towards the blandishments of reason, or East, towards the accommodation of a ridiculous faith, a yielding to heart and imagination?

John Donne (1573-1631) rounded off the sixteenth century and opened up the seventeenth. It was an era of religious turmoil, an age when poetry had just settled into a worthy manse and provided its writers with weapons to acquire either preferment at court or a short and heady stay in the Tower of London. John Donne vacillated wonderfully between religious writing and secular, between God and his Mistresses, between public service and hidden family; between east, and west.

In 1530 England had broken with Rome and a Convocation was forced to state that Henry VIII was the supreme head of the church in England. In 1534 parliament voted the king as head of the church, and the break with Rome was complete. In 1549 Cranmer's *Book of Common Prayer* appeared and was quickly imposed on the nation. In 1588 Elizabeth came to the throne and in 1599 the 'Act of Supremacy' forbade the authority of the Pope. There were decades of persecution, beheadings and heresies, violence, despair, coupled with a great humanist lift in the excitement of the renaissance, the arrival of the courtly lyric, a new grace in secular forms.

John Donne's age was an age like ours, with its wars and fevers, the turning of a century, religious doubts and affirmations. Donne's progress, as poet and believer, is exemplary of his time and his self-questioning an example to everyman. He spends his life, both in his poetry and in his prose works, preaching a sermon to himself, urging himself away from the arms of sensual pleasures and into the demanding arms of his God. A perennial struggle, sometimes won, more often lost.

John Donne was born in 1572 to a mother who came from a prominent Roman Catholic family. Two of John's uncles became members of the Society of Jesus. One of these uncles, Jasper Heywood, returned from his studies abroad to England in 1581 as a Jesuit missionary, but he was quickly captured, imprisoned, tried and condemned to the Tower. In 1584 Donne matriculated from Oxford at a time when the law demanded that those pursuing university degrees acknowledge that the king was head of the church but Donne appears to have been young enough to avoid having to take that oath. Later he studied law at Lincoln's Inn while, in 1593, his brother Henry was arrested for harbouring a Roman Catholic priest, William Harrington, in his rooms. The priest was executed and Henry died of the plague in Newgate prison.

Donne, the pragmatist, began to examine the controversy between Rome and Canterbury. The consequences of adhering to his mother's belief seemed, on the secular front, rather disquieting. He went through a period of cynicism, professing himself for a time neither one thing nor the other. While it is clear that persecution of Catholics was rife, yet his mother does not appear to have known any difficulties; John, exceptionally bright and successful in his early career, may simply have shucked off religion because it was the thing that young sparks did – and still do. He became known as a man-about-town, enjoying theatre and tavern and fair women. Swanning. His reputation as a poet grew with great speed, his love lyrics, his verse letters, his elegies, his satires. His growing reputation and the delights of high living urged him strongly to aim for court preferment.

His poetry at this stage was utterly secular, romping through witty love conceits, clever twists and turns of language, clear and mastered forms.

My face in thine eye, thine in mine appears,
And true plain hearts do in the faces rest;
Where can we find two better hemispheres
Without sharp north, without declining west?
Whatever dies, was not mix'd equally;
If our two loves be one, or thou and I
Love so alike that none can slacken, none can die.

A life lived away from reality, a life of love and of lying abed, unwilling to have the light of everyday sunshine interrupt:

Busy old fool, unruly Sun,
    Why dost thou thus,
Through windows, and through curtains, call on us?
Must to thy motions lovers' seasons run?
    Saucy pedantic wretch, go chide
    Late school-boys and sour prentices,
  Go tell court-huntsmen that the king will ride,
  Call country ants to harvest offices;
Love, all alike, no season knows nor clime,
Nor hours, days, months, which are the rags of time.

The vigour of his lines was new and profoundly memorable yet all the time he was preening himself in public, haunting the centres of worldly comfort, he remained deeply sensitive and close to his mother, remembering always her lessons and example. While seeking high office, Donne spent some time as a soldier, stating that he wished to escape the consequences of his amours, and that he wanted to earn, in service to his king, some court advancement.

Only we know, that which all Idiots say,
They bear most blows which come to part the fray.
France in her lunatic giddiness did hate

Ever our men, yea and our God of late;
Yet she relies upon our Angels well,
Which nere return; no more than they which fell.
Sick Ireland is with a strange war possessed
Like to an Ague; now raging, now at rest;
Which time will cure: yet it must do her good
If she were purg'd, and her head vayne let blood.

Poor Ireland! It would do us all a great deal of good to be purged, to have blood let out of our vacillating heads. It would do John Donne some good, too. He returned to London, disillusioned, unsuccessful, and poor, yet was given employment in the offices of Thomas Egerton, serving at court and moving, a little more quietly, in important circles. He fell in love with Ann More, whose father was one of Queen Elizabeth's favourites. She was then aged about fourteen or fifteen. He married her secretly (lest he jeopardise his chances) unknown to her family and to the court. All of this placed him in danger: marrying a minor, without the family consent, violating both canon and social laws and mores. When Sir George More eventually found out he was incensed; he had Donne sacked from his position, refused to accept the marriage and had the poor poet thrown into jail. Dear, heartsore John! And all of this for love! Sir George, thankfully, relented quickly enough but would not take in John and Ann who had to seek shelter with a friend, Sir Francis Wolley. Donne was now destitute, he was removed from society and living in near poverty. He was truly plucking the twanging strings of suffering.

For a number of years he lived quietly, visiting London often and still seeking to find favour there. By now he had seven children and both he and Ann were suffering ill health. But he had found God again! During these years he wrote that wonderful series of 'Holy Sonnets', *Oh my black soul! ... This is my play's last scene ... At the round earth's imagined corners ... Death be not proud ... Batter my heart ...* Ill-health and the awareness of the fragility of life had sobered him, yet the poems retain the vigour of language and the mastery of paradox that had lifted his love-lyrics to great heights. It is the glory of the best of the 'Holy Sonnets' that they bring the ragamuffin younger Donne before us in his very real struggles to accept what religion requires: a total commitment. His poem pleads to God to take the initiative and force Donne to be a saint!

Batter my heart, three person'd God, for you
As yet but knock, breathe, shine, and seek to mend;
That I may rise and stand, o'erthrow me' and bend
Your force, to break, blow, burn and make me new.
I, like an usurped town to another due,
Labour to' admit you, but Oh, to no end,
Reason your viceroy in me, me should defend,
But is captived, and proves weak or untrue.
Yet dearly' I love you,' and would be loved fain,
But am betroth'd unto your enemy:
Divorce me, untie, or break that knot again,
Take me to you, imprison me, for I
Except you' enthrall me, never shall be free,
Nor ever chaste, except you ravish me.

How awkward seeming, those elisions, yet how precisely they slow the run of the verses, how perfectly they mirror in sound the hesitant, yet willing movement of the soul of the poet writing them. Donne was always a consummate craftsman and it is this that gives all his goings grace, and all his entrances and exits a wily elegance.

During these years, too, Donne was participating in theological controversies and wrote a pamphlet, *Pseudo-Martyr* in 1610 where he tried to persuade Roman Catholics to accept the Oath of Allegiance. He was to take holy orders in 1615, partly urged to do so as a result of the success of his pamphlet though he hesitated for a long time, remembering his ambitions, his worldliness, his sins. It was during this time of semi-poverty, of vacillation, of living between bouts of good and ill health, that he wrote his great Good Friday poem, 1613. He was unaware that Ann was shortly to die in child-birth; he was aware of his advancing age and his own ill-health, he was aware that his opportunities for position and wealth and power were fast diminishing. The poem opens his heart to his own doubts and difficulties, hopes and sufferings, longings and weaknesses. Decisions, decisions! As in most of his best poems, Donne becomes a watcher on the battlements of himself, an actor on a stage reasoning with his own soul. This is a method of self-analysis that takes place before his public and that, at its best here, satisfies the whole man, the artist, the cynic, the lover, the religious. Beginning with the notion that a human is like a sphere, like a billiard ball perhaps, that has within himself the principle of his own movement, 'devotion'; however, if such a sphere yields to the impulses of a foreign body – like devotion to wealth, or court, or advancement – then the soul is impelled in directions other than those it ought to travel. East or west? Good Friday, a day when the heart is impelled to examine itself, the urgencies that give it motive and motion, facing the paradoxes of Christian belief and the demands that belief makes. Decisions! What are the motives that set the soul towards its goals?

Good Friday, 1613, Riding Westward
Let man's soul be a sphere, and then, in this,
Th' intelligence that moves, devotion is;
And as the other spheres, by being grown
Subject to foreign motion, lose their own,
And being by others hurried every day,
Scarce in a year their natural form obey;
Pleasure or business, so, our souls admit
For their first mover, and are whirl'd by it.
Hence is't, that I am carried towards the west,
This day, when my soul's form bends to the East.
There I should see a Sun by rising set,
And by that setting endless day beget.
But that Christ on His cross did rise and fall,
Sin had eternally benighted all.
Yet dare I almost be glad, I do not see
That spectacle of too much weight for me.
Who sees Gods face, that is self-life, must die;

What a death were it then to see God die?
It made His own lieutenant, Nature, shrink,
It made His footstool crack, and the sun wink.
Could I behold those hands, which span the poles
And tune all spheres at once, pierced with those holes?
Could I behold that endless height, which is
Zenith to us and our antipodes,
Humbled below us? or that blood, which is
The seat of all our soul's, if not of His,
Made dirt of dust, or that flesh which was worn
By God for His apparel, ragg'd and torn?
If on these things I durst not look, durst I
On His distressed Mother cast mine eye,
Who was God's partner here, and furnish'd thus
Half of that sacrifice which ransom'd us?
Though these things as I ride be from mine eye,
They're present yet unto my memory,
For that looks towards them; and Thou look'st towards me,
O Saviour, as Thou hang'st upon the tree.
I turn my back to thee but to receive
Corrections till Thy mercies bid Thee leave.
O think me worth Thine anger, punish me,
Burn off my rust, and my deformity;
Restore Thine image, so much, by Thy grace,
That Thou mayst know me, and I'll turn my face.

Preaching a Sermon to Myself

In 1623, John Donne fell seriously ill. He was then aged about fifty-one, he had lost his young and much-loved wife, he had tried, and was trying still, to come to terms with his sensual leanings. He came down with a fever which left him thoroughly weakened. It was known as the 'relapsing fever', bringing with it insomnia and prostration, as well as the usual pains associated with fever. And, of course, it was a fever into which there was every possibility he would 'relapse'. There were long periods of convalescing, giving him a good deal of time for the contemplation of our sorry human estate, something John Donne was always happy to examine, and remind himself of, in his attempts to curb the body's appetites. He would dwell more especially on humanity's more negative aspects, and most of all on death. He issued a series of what he called 'Devotions', moving from an intellectual examination of how we stand and fall, towards a deeper understanding of spiritual things. The aim of these devotions was to urge the spirit towards the love of God rather than wasting life, as he told himself he had done, in transitory loves. Perhaps the most famous quotation from Donne comes, in fact, from one of these devotions. I want to wallpaper a study of two of his greater poems with this particular devotion.

Now, This Bell Tolling Softly for Another, Says to Me: Thou Must Die
Perchance he for whom this bell tolls may be so ill, as that he knows not it tolls for him; and perchance I may think myself so much better than I am, as that they who are about me, and see my state, may have caused it to toll for me, and I know not that. The church is Catholic, universal, so are all her actions; all that she does belongs to all. When she baptises a

child, that action concerns me; for that child is thereby connected to that body which is my head, too, and ingrafted into
that body whereof I am a member. And when she buries a
man, that action concerns me: all mankind is of one author,
and is one volume; when one man dies, one chapter is not
torn out of the book, but translated into another language;
and every chapter must be so translated; God employs several
translators; some pieces are translated by age, some by sickness, some by war, some by injustice; but God's hand is in
every translation, and his hand shall bind up all our scattered
leaves again for that library where every book shall lie open
to one another.

Every poet addresses his work to somebody, most usually to
himself, and Donne's work – even, I believe his most fusty sermons – are directed to convince himself of the truths he needs to
hold. There are so many poems beginning with a call to the self
to take notice:
    'I am two fools, I know ...' 'Good we must love, and must
    hate ill ...' 'O, my black soul, now thou art summoned ...'
    'This is my play's last scene ...' 'What if this present were the
    world's last night ?' ... 'Wilt thou love God as he thee? then
    digest, My soul, this wholesome meditation' ...

In our early years on this earth, the concept of time does not
impinge that much. For John Donne, in his early, sensually-oc-
cupied years, time was both a joy (when he was with his lover)
and a bitch (when they had to part). Thus even his early poems
are alert to antinomy and paradox:
    Now thou hast loved me one whole day,
    To-morrow when thou leavest, what wilt thou say? ...

    Love, all alike, no season knows nor clime,
    Nor hours, days, months, which are the rags of time ...

    For every hour that thou wilt spare me now,
        I will allow,
    Usurious god of love, twenty to thee,
    When with my brown my gray hairs equal be ...

Having secretly married the under-age Ann More, Donne found himself in jail, thrown out of his job, rejected by the parents of his young bride. In one of his 'secular' poems, in an effort to get his lover to be more condescending to his wishes he wrote: ('The Flea')

O stay, three lives in one flea spare,
Where we almost, yea, more than married are.
This flea is you and I, and this
Our marriage bed, and marriage temple is.
Though parents grudge, and you, we're met,
And cloister'd in these living walls of jet.

She goes on to 'purple her nail' with the blood of the flea, thus killing three at one go: because the flea had sucked his blood, and then hers:

Just so much honour, when thou yield'st to me,
Will waste, as this flea's death took life from thee.

The point of the writing is in the writing itself, the pleasure is in the argument, the humour, the serious fun. Donne wrote a great deal of wonderful poetry in like vein, witty, reasonable, filled with paradox and paradigm. Until life hurt him, and death. His beloved Ann died in child-birth, leaving Donne perplexed and stricken. When he eventually got the preferment in court that he had longed for and laboured towards, a high seriousness had taken over. In 1621 he was made Dean of St Paul's. In the later years of his life he became well-known as a preacher. As he still suffered regular bouts of serious illness, death was constantly before his mind and two of his most perfect religious poems, *Hymn to God the Father* and *Hymn to God my God, in my Sickness*, were written. And even here, in these late, great poems, Donne will not resist the temptation to a little bit of verbal trickery and fun. It is this dexterity with language that makes the poetry strike home to the rest of us, who tend to resent any high seriousness if it is not gently sauced with wit and humour. Indeed, the point of Donne's sermons and poems is that they are addressed to himself as well as, and as much as to an audience, and this sense of being a watcher and a hearer rather than the one addressed, takes the reader unawares and wins assent the more readily.

As therefore the bell that rings to a sermon calls not upon the preacher only, but upon the congregation to come, so this bell calls us all; but how much more me, who am brought so near the door by this sickness. There was a contention as far as a suit (in which both piety and dignity, religion and esti- mation, were mingled), which of the religious orders should ring to prayers first in the morning; and it was determined, that they should ring first that rose earliest. If we understand aright the dignity of this bell that tolls for our evening prayer, we should be glad to make it ours by rising early, in that appli- cation, that it might be ours as well as his, whose indeed it is.

In January of 1631 Donne's mother died. He had been caring for her for some time, a fact which seems to show that she and Donne, in spite of his removal from her Roman Catholic faith, never really lost trust in one another. He died very soon after her, in March of the same year. The intensity of his seriousness in later life as he pursued his calling as a divine goes some way to dissolve the complaint that his dismissal of the Roman faith was done out of fear of imprisonment at that time. But he did not come to God all complete in his devotion, all saucered and blowed, all prepared for divine love.

Hymne to God My God, in My Sickness
Since I am coming to that Holy roome,
     Where, with thy Choir of Saints for evermore,
I shall be made thy Music; As I come
       I tune the Instrument at the dore,
       And what I must do then, think here before.

Whilst my Physicians by their love are growne
     Cosmographers, and I their Map, who lie
Flat on this bed, that by them may be shown
       That this is my South-west discoverie
       Per fretum febris, by these streights to die,

I joy, that in these straits, I see my West;
    For, though their currents yield return to none,
What shall my West hurt me? As West and East
    In all flatt Maps (and I am one) are one,
    So death doth touch the Resurrection.

Is the Pacific Sea my home? Or are
    The Eastern riches? Is *Jerusalem*?
Anyan, and *Magellan*, and *Gibraltar*,
    All streights, and none but streights, are ways to them,
    Whether where *Japhet* dwells, or *Cham*, or *Sem*.

We think that *Paradise* and *Calvary*,
    Christ's Crosse, and *Adam's* tree, stood in one place;
Look Lord, and find both *Adams* met in me;
    As the first *Adam's* sweat surrounds my face,
    May the last *Adam's* blood my soule embrace.

So, in his purple wrapp'd receive me Lord,
    By these his thorns give me his other Crown;
And as to others soules I preached thy word,
    Be this my Text, my Sermon to mine own,
Therefore that he may raise the Lord throws down.

Here is the poet urging himself to prepare for imminent death: *What I must do then, think here before.* This is high serious-ness to begin with, but it is directed to himself, a warning, a warning that moves on, however, through his delight in the play on words, 'strait' and 'straight', to develop his theme in playful seriousness. Lying on his back in bed he sees himself as a map of the world, laid out flat, the West therefore tipping the East, and (as in the great poem *Good Friday, 1613, Riding Westward*) death and resurrection also are seen to tip each other. This 'conceit', in its wit and accuracy, convinces Donne and convinces the reader, during the time the poem is being absorbed, because of the strength and serious ongoing flow of the stanzas. It must be re-membered that Donne was writing in a time when religious con-troversy was something new and intense, and did not bother too

much about the accuracy of the statements he might make in the
second last stanza. What matters here is Donne's effort, by using
words and music and paradox, his beloved tools, to convince
himself of what he wants to believe. And all of it moving inex-
orably to the final line, itself the ultimate paradox which is here
stated in simple terms, without strain or anxiety in the monosyl-
lables, resulting in a resolution of his sorry state.

In the poetry of John Donne, as he gradually moved from
human, sexual love to the love of God, there is a delicate growth
in trust and faith, indeed in joy, in spite of all Donne's physical
ailments. The shift to religious poetry is indeed so delicate that
the sensual imagery that gave zest to the early poetry, turns into
the imagery of the joy of the Lord. The shift towards a trust in
the spiritual grows easily and organically out of his zeal for the
natural man. Donne's religion is far from being that of a dour
Anglican clergyman, nor of a Calvinist disgusted with natural
things, but is rich in awareness that the natural things of life are
even more wonderful when underpinned by the grace of God.
Yet Donne was conscious of sin and guilt, of how a sinner falls
over and over again, and is forgiven over and over again. It is, in
Donne, a constant cycle of falling, of repentance and forgiveness, of falling again. In God's continual willingness to forgive
Donne finds his joy; in his own continual willingness to fall,
Donne finds he has to keep reminding himself of God's mercy,
he has to keep preaching a sermon to himself. He has to come to
terms with his sensual and sinful self in terms of his newfound
faith in the love of God; as he would say to himself, I have not
yet got John Donne settled: *When I have done, I have not done ...* If
his earlier poems were written with an eye to an audience of
bright young things, both male and female, at court, the later
poems take on more of an awareness of an audience that he
wants to lead through to eternal life, the main person in that audience being himself. Donne develops a spirituality that is
deeply involved with the natural man, aware of lust and of sickness, of wars and natural disasters, and it is this down-to-earth
spirituality that still touches us deeply today.

Wilt thou forgive that sinne which I did shunne
  A yeare, or two: but wallow'd in, a score?

The bell doth toll for him that thinks it doth; and though it in-
termit again, yet from that minute that that occasion wrought
upon him, he is united to God. Who casts not up his eye to
the sun when it rises? but who takes off his eye from a comet
when that breaks out? Who bends not his ear to any bell
which upon any occasion rings? but who can remove it from
that bell which is passing a piece of himself out of this world?
No man is an island, entire of itself; every man is a piece of
the continent, a part of the main. If a clod be washed away by
the sea, Europe is the less, as well as if a promontory were, as
well as if a manor of thy friend's or of thine own were: any
man's death diminishes me, because I am involved in
mankind, and therefore never send to know for whom the
bell tolls; it tolls for thee ...

Donne, in his early poetry, used paradox to great effect, in-
jecting the humour of his quiet but certain wit. Later he came to
see that the God he was growing more and more to believe and
trust in was a God of paradox. 'That He may raise, the Lord
throws down.' Nor is it possible to resolve this paradox. 'To
whom God gives more, of him He requires more.' In a sermon
he called 'Christ the Light', preached at St Paul's Cathedral on
Christmas Day, 1621, he developed the light and darkness paradox. 'In all philosophy,' he told his riveted listeners, 'there is not
so dark a thing as light.' Indeed, Donne had come to see living itself as paradoxical – in the midst of life we are in death. In that
sermon he said: 'He that should come to a heathen man, a mere
natural man, uncatechised, uninstructed in the rudiments of the
Christian religion, and should at first, without any preparation,
present him first with this necessity: that thou shalt burn in fire
and brimstone eternally except thou believe in a Trinity of persons, in an unity of one God, except thou believe that a virgin
had a son and the same Son that God had, and that God was
man too and being the immortal God yet died, he should be so

far from working any spiritual cure upon this poor soul, as that
he should rather bring Christian mysteries into scorn than him
to a belief. For that man, if you proceed so (believe all or you
burn in hell), would find an easy, an obvious way to escape all;
that is, first not to believe in hell itself, and then nothing would
bind him to believe the rest.'

The paradoxes on which the foundations of the whole
Christian faith rest brought John Donne face to face with his
own excitement over language, and his own utter dread of
death. His poetry, and his sermons, urged himself on to an acceptance of the God of love, light and life, who brings us down
into darkness and death so that that love can be fulfilled.

In his sermon preached at St Paul's in 1625 he said: 'All our
life is a continual burden, yet we must not groan; a continual
squeezing, yet we must not pant. And as in the tenderness of our
childhood we suffer, and yet are whipped if we cry, so we are
complained of if we complain, and made delinquents if we call
the times ill. And that which adds weight to weight and multi-
plies the sadness of this consideration is this: that still the best
men have had the most laid upon them.' And there is the great
'Death's Duell' sermon, preached during Lent 1630 at Whitehall
in the presence of King Charles I. Here, at last, there is resolution
of enigma, there is melding of antinomies, a breathing away of
paradox, all in the awareness of the unconditional love of God.
'... it is in his power to give us an issue and deliverance, even
then when we are brought to the jaws and teeth of death, and to
the lips of that whirlpool, the grave.' This is the final paradox,
that we shall find 'a deliverance in death. Not that God will de-
liver us from dying, but that he will have a care of us in the hour
of death, of what kind soever our passage be ...' 'We have a
winding sheet in our mother's womb, which grows with us from
our conception, and we come into the world, wound up in that
winding sheet, for we come to seek a grave.' 'How much worse a
death than death is this life, which so good men would so often
change for death!' Contemplating our death he speaks with Job,
'Corruption thou art my father,' and he says to the worm, 'Thou

art my mother and my sister'. And goes on, with great relish:
'Miserable riddle, when the same worm must be my mother and
my sister and myself. Miserable incest, when I must be married
to my mother and my sister, and be both father and mother to
my own mother and sister, begat and bear that worm which is
all that miserable penury.' These are the resolutions that lead
him to his last great poem:

A Hymne to God the Father
I
Wilt thou forgive that sinne where I begunne,
  Which is my sin, though it were done before?
Wilt thou forgive those sinnes through which I runne,
  And do run still: though still I do deplore?
    When thou hast done, thou hast not done,
      For I have more.

II
Wilt thou forgive that sinne by which I'have wonne
  Others to sinne? and, made my sinne their doore?
Wilt thou forgive that sinne which I did shunne
  A yeare, or two: but wallow'd in, a score?
    When thou hast done, thou hast not done,
      For I have more.

III
I have a sinne of feare, that when I have spunne
  My last thred, I shall perish on the shore;
But sweare by thy self, that at my death thy sonne
  Shall shine as he shines now, and heretofore;
    And, having done that, thou hast done,
      I have no more.

The poems lead up to this moment, 'I have a sin of feare, that
when I have spunne / My last thread, I shall perish on the
shore'. The tone of this poem is playful and, given the theme,
this playfulness underscores a trust and hope, an ease with his
faith, a certainty that forgiveness will be there and he will be

taken past the shore and into heaven. He has persuaded himself, through his poetry and his dealing with a difficult and painful life, that God is there, is loving, forgiving, and has overcome death. And all this has been achieved with the help of an understanding of paradox in that faith, and a joyful use of the paradoxes with which language is rich and rife.

Neither can we call this a begging of misery, or a borrowing of misery, as though we were not miserable enough of ourselves, but must fetch in more from the next house, in taking upon us the misery of our neighbours. Truly it were an excusable covetousness if we did, for affliction is a treasure, and scarce any man hath enough of it. No man hath affliction enough that is not matured and ripened by it, and made fit for God by that affliction. If a man carry treasure in bullion, or in a wedge of gold, and have none coined into current money, his treasure will not defray him as he travels. Tribulation is treasure in the nature of it, but it is not current money in the use of it, except we get nearer and nearer our home, heaven, by it. And another man may be sick too, and sick to death, and this affliction may lie in his bowels, as gold in a mine, and be of no use to him; but this bell, that tells me of his affliction, digs out and applies that gold to me: if by this consideration of another's danger I take mine own into contemplation, and so secure myself, by making my recourse to my God, who is our only security.

To Keep a True Lent

Robert Herrick (1591-1674)

Is this a Fast, to keep
  The larder lean?
   And clean
From fat of veals and sheep?

Is it to quit the dish
  Of flesh, yet still
   To fill
The platter high with fish?

Is it to fast an hour,
  Or ragg'd to go,
   Or show
A down-cast look and sour?

No: 'tis a Fast to dole
  Thy sheaf of wheat
   And meat
Unto the hungry soul.

It is to fast from strife
  And old debate,
   And hate;
To circumcise thy life.

To show a heart grief-rent;
  To starve thy sin,
   Not bin;
And that's to keep thy Lent.

Guilty of Dust

George Herbert in the Light of Simone Weil

Behold, thy dust doth stir,
It moves, it creeps, it aims at thee:
   Wilt thou defer
   To succor me,
Thy pile of dust, wherein each crumb
    Says, Come?
(Longing)

George Herbert was born in Montgomery, Wales in 1593. His father died when George was very young and he and his six brothers and three sisters were raised by their mother, patron to John Donne who dedicated his 'Holy Sonnets' to her. George studied at Trinity College, Cambridge. When Herbert's mother died in 1627, her funeral sermon was delivered by John Donne. Herbert took his degrees and was elected a major fellow of Trinity; in 1618 he was appointed Reader in Rhetoric at Cambridge, and in 1620 he was elected public orator. This was a special honour and, in an attempt to serve his king, whom he saw as promoting peace and justice, he had himself elected, in 1624, to represent Montgomery in parliament. He was quickly disillusioned with parliament and found he could serve his God better in the priesthood. In 1629, Herbert married his step-father's cousin Jane Danvers.

He took holy orders in the Church of England in 1630 and spent the rest of his life as rector in Bemerton near Salisbury. Here he preached and wrote poetry, helped rebuild the church out of his own funds and cared deeply for his parishioners. He came to be known as 'Holy Mr Herbert' around the countryside in the three years before his death of consumption, at the too-early age of forty, in 1633. Reading his poems over and over, one gets the impression that here is a man whose every thought focuses on his God, whose every mood is examined in the light of God's love, God's presence or absence, whose every sense of failing blames the self as a being composed merely of dust, whose every hope is that this dust will be resurrected by a God who becomes, not a remote and angry figure, but a friend, closer than any human being can ever be.

Anthony Thwaite called Herbert 'the chief ornament of the Anglican Church'. His writings were not published in his lifetime but he left them to the care of his friend and fellow parson, Nicholas Ferrar of Little Gidding, asking him to publish the poems only if he thought they might do good to 'any dejected poor soul'.

W. H. Auden said of him that 'one does not get the impression from his work that the temptations of the flesh were a serious spiritual menace to him, as they were to Donne.' This, of course, we do not know but it seems clear from the poems and from his prose passages outlining the ideals he had for the parson, 'The Country Pastor', that he did attempt to keep his life in perfect order. Nor did he seem to suffer from religious doubts: in the seventeenth century very few people did. Herbert's struggles were interior ones, debating in his own heart with God and with his own human appetites. Above all the awareness was one of human frailty and hopelessness without the intervention of a loving God.

George Herbert comes across, then, as someone who has worked it all out. It is he, perhaps, who best exemplifies the dangers and the successes of writing out of a generally shared store of images and references, and out of a widely accepted and understood set of beliefs. The dangers are mainly those of sermonising, banality, of repeating oneself *ad nauseam*, of speaking out of a sense of belonging to a church that has the monopoly of truth. And I am afraid that I find Herbert does all of this, his work often becoming little more than flat and stultifying hymn-pushing. His successes, and they are very many, come when he takes off his priestly robes, the masks of preacher, the make-up and costume of guide, and faces his God with direct intent, focusing on his own experience as suffering man face to face with a God who is undoubtedly there but fades too often behind the dust-grimed windows of the human mind. How touchingly honest these lines: 'Thou that has given so much to me,/Give one thing more, a grateful heart.' Yet how painful is the sermonising:

Drink not the third glass, which thou canst not tame,
When once it is within thee; but before
Mayst rule it, as thou list; and poure the shame,
Which it would pour on thee, upon the floor.

I'm not sure too many pubs and inns, nor too many salons, would appreciate your doing just that. Occasionally, too, his taste is questionable:

The brags of life are but a nine days' wonder;
    And after death the fumes that spring
From private bodies, make as big a thunder,
    As those which rise from a huge King.

Sometimes his views on woman are not so wholesome: 'Who, when he is to treat/With sick folks, women, those whom passions sway,/Allows for that, and keeps his constant way.' His Christ, however, is a real, a human person, close to the sufferings of humanity and close to the author's heart and mind, dining with thieves, laying tables for meals, and to whom Herbert refers as 'my dear'. This at times easy intimacy is a delight in religious verse and surfaces again in Hopkins, centuries later, in both its delightful and terrible forms.

Apart from the decorum and decency of his fine verses, Herbert's ongoing appeal lies in his argument, not with God or with himself, but with an inherent 'guilt' in humankind that leads him inevitably to destruction. This is the entropy that Teilhard de Chardin later took to its extremes; it is what Herbert calls being 'guilty of dust', and it is that phrase, and the poem in which it abides, that appears to me to be one of the most compelling of all great religious poems. Its shortness hides the depth and range of its thought and experience; its perfect form hides the deep and ongoing experience the author brings to the work.

And here's a passage from 'The Country Parson', not too cheerful, nor too promising: 'The Country Parson is generally sad, because he knows nothing but the Cross of Christ, his mind being defixed on it with those nails wherewith his Master was: or if he have any leisure to look off from thence, he meets continually with two most sad spectacles, Sin, and Misery; God dishonoured every day, and man afflicted.' Which sorry passage brings me to the core of my approach to Herbert: through the work of Simone Weil, to the great poem *Love*. I am not suggesting that Simone Weil was moved by Herbert's poetry and of course I am not suggesting that Herbert foresaw the writings of Simone Weil! But great thinkers, great writers, I believe, touch on something essential and permanent in the life of the earth, and therefore their works may often clarify one another. This is my hope in the area of Herbert's poetry, leading to that great, dramatically beautiful and hugely inclusive poem.

The basic groundwork of Simone Weil's thinking, in so far as I understand the writing, is that man is a sinful creature. He needs redemption. This is achieved, firstly by Christ's grace, offered without our meriting it, but redemption is also by reduction and annihilation of the ego, by 'decreation'. She sees God as utter perfection, living in eternal fullness, without need or desire and then yielding that perfection in the act of creating, as an act of supreme love, and a diminution of his own being. In this way, God's act in creating is an act of renunciation and abdication. In this fullness of God's vision, Christ the Son would need to suffer and die, so to enter most completely into the living, suffering and dying of human beings, thereby sharing everything and thereby, too, redeeming everything to that creating God; and so, she says, 'The crucifixion of God is an eternal thing.' It is not God's power, but his love, that fuels the universe, the diminution of self when he creates being nothing less than a perfect act of love. As renunciation then God is love; as might and power, in the creation of the material universe, its ongoing thrust and development and its necessary entropy and construction/destruction, he remains undiminished. There exists a space therefore between God and God, between love and transcendence; it is this space that must be filled by a loving humanity. Christ stands like a beggar imploring humanity for this love.

God's creating power Weil sees as 'necessity', the impulsion without which everything would be static throughout creation. God as power is the terrible and indifferent onward thrust of creation, a thrust that may be violent, in earthquake, tsunami, hurricane, meteorite; it is blind, mathematical, implacable and often cruel. Without such a motion, however, God as love would not be available to us. This impulse to growth and change is present everywhere in creation and is present, too, in man. Necessity in itself has no moral connotations and God does not interfere (*pace* miracles!) in its ongoing thrust. This is what the Stoics saw as fate, or destiny, a purely arbitrary and indifferent force that urges creation to its growth. Here, I believe, is the force which makes Herbert speak of man as 'guilty of dust'.

'God created because he was good, but the creature let itself be created because it was evil. It redeemed itself by persuading God through endless entreaties to destroy it.' (Weil) In creating human beings, God gave them something unique: free will and autonomy. He created us with the freedom to accept and return, or to reject his love. For what is love if it is not given freely? Weil sees this autonomy as the great sorrow in human living because the human will is weak, it is not obedient to God as the growth of a flower is obedient to God's creating ordinance. Hence, in failing in obedience, man fails in love; he is, then, guilty of sin. If, however, man's autonomy is renounced, if it is given back to God in a free gesture of total obedience, then man becomes fully in tune with God's love in creating. To do this, however, is to refuse autonomy; it is to become saints almost beyond sainthood; it is, virtually, impossible. At the root of Weil's thinking, then, is this despair. 'Decreation', a necessary movement in the human will, is impossible. The closer mankind comes to the obedience of material things, the closer is man's will to God's.

Human beings, then, stand before God as before a mirror; when they peer at God, they see but themselves, and often they see themselves as they wish to see themselves. Nature, on the other hand, stands before God as before a clear glass; you can see through it to God himself. Weil sees the use of free will as a 'sin'; 'Evil,' she says, 'is the distance between the creature and God.' Is it any wonder she suffered so much in her own life and eventually, through a final act of decreating herself, lost her life at a young age?

'By the effect of grace, little by little the I disappears, and God loves himself through the creature who becomes empty, who becomes nothing.' Egotism and egocentrism form a screen before God's creation: 'The ego is only the shadow projected by sin and error which blocks God's light and which I take for a being.' Man's response to God must be on two levels, one, love, the other, acceptance; love of God as our creator and redeemer, and acceptance of the necessary thrust of the universe. Failure in these means being guilty of sin and guilty, as Herbert puts it, of dust. Love, as Weil saw it, is the unreserved consent to the existence of the world and of other human beings, and it corresponds to the sacrificial generosity of God as love, of Christ.

Now, the poems of George Herbert. He is aware of the great generosity of the creating God. Many of his poems tell of the need for man to respond to that generosity. As in the following poem where the title suggests 'reprise' of a theme, the theme of gratitude to God for what he has done for us.

The Reprisal

    I have consider'd it, and find
There is no dealing with thy mighty passion:
For though I die for thee, I am behind;
    My sins deserve the condemnation.

    Oh make me innocent, that I
May give a disentangled state and free:
And yet thy wounds still my attempts defy,
    For by thy death I die for thee.

Ah! was it not enough that thou
By thy eternal glory didst outgo me?
Couldst thou not grief's sad conquests me allow,
But in all vict'ries overthrow me?

Yet by confession will I come
Into the conquest. Though I can do nought
Against thee, in thee I will overcome
The man, who once against thee fought.

Herbert sees man as guilty, and deserving of punishment and death. It is the overwhelming love of God that throws man down, suggesting both the paucity of man's response, and the generosity of that same God that gives some hope. He begins his prose treatise, 'The Country Pastor' by saying: 'A Pastor is the Deputy of Christ for the reducing of Man to the Obedience of God.' It is this failure in obedience that brings man to sin. R. S. Thomas says of Herbert's own and frequent illnesses: 'In fact Herbert like a good Anglican equates sickness with sin, and good health with holiness, believing implicitly in God's power to heal, if it be also his will.'

Herbert wrote out of the tradition, but his grasp of it was imaginative, each poem carefully wrought and well-proportioned, and finely structured. This very structuring into carefully crafted forms fitting each individual poem, echoes in itself an ordering imagination that works out of surety and the delights of constraint; some poems are didactic, arguments with others, but the best are interior arguments with self and not on doubts but on self-doubt. Those poems, like Love, which are fully achieved, have about them a sense of the special love of Christ for the soul in their very many song-like qualities.

There is, then, the question of dust! In the poem Easter, speaking to his own heart that it should sing the Lord's praise he says:

That, as his death calcined thee to dust,
His life may make thee gold, and much more just.

Jesus' death is seen as burning down to ashes the heart of

man, yet out of these ashes, this dust, gold may be retrieved. The
natural progress of man, then, is to die, as Jesus did, to become
dust, but because of Jesus' resurrection, dust is no longer the
final end of man's life. In *Easter Wings* mankind is seen as
'Decaying more and more'; if, however, a man can grow in harmony with the Christ, and rise in praise at his resurrection, then
the impetus towards destruction can become its opposite
through grace. 'Then shall the fall further the flight in me.' For
this reason, when Herbert uses the word 'dust' at the end of a
line, seeking a rhyme he will most often use the word 'trust'. The
opposite seems true, also; when the sense of sin prevails, then he
will rhyme 'dust' with 'lust' which often takes the place, in
Herbert's language, of the generic term 'sin'. He will see 'sick-
nesses and shame' as God's punishment for sin, and in this case
being guilty of dust and guilty of sin are close aligned: yet, turning to God again a similar line will prevail: 'Affliction shall advance the flight in me.'

The way towards trust is to go with the will of God; 'Let me
be soft and supple to thy will.' In a poem called *Holy Baptism*
Herbert writes:

> The growth of flesh is but a blister,
>> Childhood is health.

Apart from its possible influence on the thinking of Henry
Vaughan, this too shows how closely Herbert equated physical
and spiritual well-being. All through the poetry it is the undeserved love Christ offers the soul that carries the soul through to
eternal life: the individual, without God's grace, cannot succeed.
Man's natural inclination is to 'die, or fight, or travel, or deny';
man's heart is naturally filled with 'venom':

> Oh smooth my rugged heart, and there
> Engrave thy rev'rend law and fear;
> Or make a new one, since the old
>> Is sapless grown,
>> And a much fitter stone
> To hide my dust, than thee to hold.

In the poem *Sin*, he outlines the ways and means God has devised to guide the soul, from the care of parents, through the methods the church herself employs, to angels and grace:

Yet all these fences, and their whole array
One cunning bosom-sin blows quite away.

One cunning bosom-sin! For Herbert, a man properly ordered in every aspect of his life, from his health, through his manner of dress, to his reverent approach to God in prayer, has the greatest hope of countering the disorder of sin and dust.

Prayer

Prayer the Church's banquet, Angels' age,
    God's breath in man returning to his birth,
    The soul in paraphrase, heart in pilgrimage,
The Christian plummet sounding heav'n and earth;

Engine against th'Almighty, sinners' tower,
    Reversed thunder, Christ-side-piercing spear,
    The six-days world transposing in an hour,
A kind of tune, which all things hear and fear;

Softness, and peace, and joy, and love, and bliss,
    Exalted Manna, gladness of the best,
    Heaven in ordinary, man well drest,
The milky way, the bird of Paradise,

Church-bells beyond the stars heard, the soul's blood,
The land of spices, something understood.

It is the sense of undeserved grace, the awareness of God's freely offered and unconditional love that touches Herbert to the core. Can man's response, in spite of his sin, in spite of his thundering towards dust, be to love in return? And what kind of love is that to be? In the poem *Christmas* Herbert speaks of Christ as 'my dear'. In the poem *Love* (I) he contrasts Love with 'that dust which thou hast made'. God made the great universe out of love, mankind has offered this 'dust' its love, giving to the creation what it should give to the creator. In *Love* (II), if Immortal Love is Heat, this poem develops the image of love as fire; if we are consumed then 'Our eyes shall see thee, which before saw dust.' Both these sonnets in some form contrast God's great creating impulse out of love with man's offering his love to the material side of creation; man, being 'a crumb of dust' ('The Temper') offers his love to dust, instead of to Love himself.

While the soul is at its devotions, the flesh is in close proximity to tombs in the poem called *Church Monuments*; 'that it betimes / May take acquaintance of this heap of dust', to which 'school' all will at last be driven. Here the earth itself is seen merely as a monument to 'death's incessant motion',

Which dissolution sure death best discern,

Comparing dust with dust, and earth with earth.

We all share, then, in this good fellowship of dust. By acquainting the body, through the mind's urgings, with its inevitable end, 'thou mayest know / That flesh is but the glass, which holds the dust, / That measures all our time; which also shall / Be crumbled into dust.' The image of the hourglass here is the perfect one for de Chardin's entropy. Twice in this poem the word 'dust' is made to rhyme with 'trust'; in the final stanza it rhymes again, this time with 'lust'. In several other poems these same rhymes recur; as already noted, it is when the emphasis is on man's sinfulness then it will rhyme with lust; when, however, there is hope in the Christ's redeeming powers, the word will rhyme with 'trust'.

Virtue

Sweet day, so cool, so calm, so bright,
The bridal of the earth and sky:
The dew shall weep thy fall tonight;
    For thou must die.

Sweet rose, whose hue angry and brave
Bids the rash gazer wipe his eye:
Thy root is ever in its grave,
    And thou must die.

Sweet spring, full of sweet days and roses,
A box where sweets compacted lie;
My music shows ye have your closes,
      And all must die.

Only a sweet and virtuous soul,
Like season'd timber, never gives;
But though the whole world turn to coal,
      Then chiefly lives.

Here the word 'coal' must be seen as cinders, ashes, dust. The poem is itself a full disclosure of how we are 'guilty of dust'. The guilt comes because we have turned our love to the created thing and not the creator. All of this is subsumed in Simone Weil's consciousness of the human condition though here it is expressed instinctively and with different emphases. If Weil's sense is of the difference of God and of man's inadequacies, how the human must move away from self into 'decreation', Herbert indeed urges man, himself, to come closer in affection and love to Christ, the great Lover. So many poems begin as familiar conversations or have lines within them that speak directly to God as a close, a very close, friend: *'My love, my sweetness, hear!'; 'My God, I read this day ...' 'Ah my dear angry Lord ...' 'My God, if writings may ...'* This easy confidence in the presence of his God underlines Herbert's sense of God as love, as Love, as close and concerned. 'Oh my Redeemer dear, / After all this canst thou be strange?' In the great poem to which I have been leading, all of these movements and ideas come together in overwhelming, yet simple majesty, a simplicity and directness that Simone Weil herself must have treasured. Man is guilty, of dust and of sin, yet it is God's very urging that insists that the response of man, even under such drawbacks, must be love, an un-guilty love.

An addendum: Jesus 'sat down and dined' with sinners, with the outcast of Jewish society, with beggars, the poor, the crippled, the blind, the lame, with the despised and ostracised, the tax collectors. He entertained sinners in his home, and was entertained by them. There is the rich parable of the wedding feast

to which the wealthy refused to come; it may well have been a
distinct memory from Jesus' own life, knowing they would not
come because the outcast might also be there. There is the story
of Jesus inviting himself to the home of Zacchaeus, the tax col-
lector, the most maligned of them all. This dining with the sinners set Jesus apart at once and showed how God himself forgave sinners, indeed went further and sought them out. The invitation to sup with Christ, then, is a very special one, relevant
as background to this dramatic poem of Herbert's, relevant, too,
to all those invitations to the table of the Lord that Christians of
all denominations are party to. Down all the ages, this inviting
of the poor and sinners to one's table has been and remains a
very uncommon thing; no doubt it was so in Herbert's time, too.
The more unusual the invitation, the more powerful looms this
poem.

Love

Love bade me welcome, yet my soul drew back,
    Guilty of dust and sin.
But quick-ey'd Love, observing me grow slack
    From my first entrance in,
Drew nearer to me, sweetly questioning,
    If I lack'd anything.

A guest, I answer'd, worthy to be here.
    Love said, You shall be he.
I the unkind, ungrateful? Ah my dear,
    I cannot look on thee.
Love took my hand, and smiling did reply,
    Who made the eyes but I?

Truth Lord, but I have marr'd them: let my shame
    Go where it doth deserve.
And know you not, says Love, who bore the blame?
    My dear, then I will serve.
You must sit down, says Love, and taste my meat:
    So I did sit and eat.

John Milton (1608-1658)

On His Blindness

When I consider how my light is spent
  Ere half my days, in this dark world and wide,
  And that one talent which is death to hide,
  Lodged with me useless, though my soul more bent
To serve therewith my Maker, and present
  My true account, lest He returning chide;
  'Doth God exact day-labour, light denied?'
  I fondly ask; but Patience, to prevent
That murmur, soon replies: 'God doth not need
  Either man's work, or His own gifts; who best
  Bear His mild yoke, they serve Him best: His state
Is kingly; thousands at His bidding speed,
  And post o'er land and ocean without rest;
  They also serve who only stand and wait.

On His Deceased Wife

Methought I saw my late espousèd saint
　Brought to me like Alcestis from the grave,
　Whom Jove's great son to her glad husband gave,
　Rescued from death by force, though pale and faint.
Mine, as whom washed from spot of child-bed taint
　Purification in the old law did save;
　And such, as yet once more I trust to have
　Full sight of her in heav'n without restraint,
Came vested all in white, pure as her mind:
　Her face was veiled, yet to my fancied sight
　Love, sweetness, goodness, in her person shined
So clear, as in no face with more delight.
　But oh! as to embrace me she inclined,
　I waked, she fled, and day brought back my night.

Dressed, and On My Way

Henry Vaughan (1622-1695)

The word 'mystic' and its adjective 'mystical' are perhaps the most misused words when it comes to poets who immerse their work in religious thought and imagery, and Henry Vaughan is probably the most subject to this too-facile use. If he stretches his being away from this world towards God, it is not in the way of sheer love or devotion; it is urged from a basis of distaste for this world and its propensity to sin, suffering and misery. A true mystic takes God as friend, even as lover, and sighs to be with God for God's sake, not out of distaste for this world. The great focus of Vaughan's poetry is on the innocence of children and childhood, combined with the notion that the child comes from the hand of God the Creator and moves away further and further from that God as life develops. The same can be said of mankind as a whole; as men and women were expelled from the Garden of Paradise and forced into the misery of human history, gradually humanity moved further from that same God. Vaughan's notion is that it would be wonderful to find a way of living in that time of innocence once more. From these ideas there spring some wonderfully beautiful poems but taken on its own merit this is not a mystical poetry, indeed it often smacks of a wish to move away from the responsibilities a person has to the self and to humanity as a whole.

That world of childhood, he believes, is close to the world of the angels who, in turn, are the closest to God. Vaughan would wish to be an angel, but again it is to escape the misery of this world. 'Since all that age doth teach, is ill ...' From all of this, too, spring the images he will employ, the basic one being that the world is darkness, the next world and God are light. Although I would substitute the word 'escapism' for the commonly used 'mysticism' when referring to Vaughan, this is in no way to denigrate the value of many of the poems that he bequeathed us.

94

In his preface to the 1655 edition of his book, he complains of poems written merely for wit's sake: 'Where the sun is busy upon a dung-hill, the issue is always some unclean vermin.' He gives credit to George Herbert with turning his own work away from mere worldly thoughts to divine things. The influence is obvious and pervasive, in phrase and image, yet Vaughan moves in a very different direction. This is a poetry of awe – more addressed to God the Father and Creator, and the One who draws all things to himself, than to his Son, a personal Friend and Soul-mate. He is a poet of innocence: not a poet guilty of dust and sin. Perhaps because the religious longing and the almost complete disheartening he knew before the world, pushed his work to take more care over the religious aspect than the poetic; therefore many of his poems are dull and repetitive, and the metaphorical fabric becomes a little threadbare from overuse.

His reading of Herbert set him off, as he admits moving from the things of the world to the light of the world to come. Light is the omnipresent image. His effort is away from the physical towards the transcendental. The influence of Herbert is everywhere palpable, in so many ways, both formal, in metaphor, and in many of his abrupt openings. Compare, for instance, the opening of his poem *The Resolve*:

I have considered it; and find
> A longer stay
Is but excused neglect.

with Herbert's opening to his poem *The Reprisal*:
I have considered it, and find
There is no dealing with thy mighty passion:

There is a poem written to Herbert, *The Match*:
Dear friend! whose holy, ever-living lines
> Have done much good
To many, and have checked my blood,
My fierce, wild blood that still heaves, and inclines,
> But is still tamed

By those bright fires which thee inflamed;
Here I join hands, and thrust my stubborn heart
Into thy deed,
There from no duties to be freed,
And if hereafter youth, or folly thwart
And claim their share,
Here I renounce the poisonous ware.

The influence of Herbert does occasionally too much intrude but it is important for Vaughan that this be continually set aside as both poets part company in so many other ways. Now and again he uses a phrase of some endearment when touching on God, such as 'Haste, haste my dear', but it does not have the same sense of genuine closeness that Herbert achieves. Herbert lives far more contentedly in, and committed to, the actual world; Vaughan despises the world and lives only for the next:

Rise to prevent the sun; sleep doth sins glut,
And heaven's gate opens, when this world's is shut.
(Rules and Lessons)

In the poem *Corruption* he sees mankind in its early years as being still so close to creation and the Creator, and to the Eden from which it was expelled, that everywhere about him, mankind catches glimpses of that glory;

Angels lay leiger here; each bush, and cell,
Each oak, and high-way knew them,
Walk but the fields, or sit down at some well,
And he was sure to view them.

A poem called *Child-hood* has these lines:

An age of mysteries! which he
Must live twice, that would God's face see;
Which Angels guard, and with it play,
Angels! which foul men drive away.

It is, of course, close to the words of Christ who said 'Suffer the little children to come to me and do not forbid them, for of such is the Kingdom of God.' From here, and from Vaughan's

intention of holding his place until he reaches death, comes that
great longing for innocence and childhood that echoes later on
in Blake and in Wordsworth, and nowhere does Vaughan
achieve a higher and more rhythmically perfect expression of
this desire than in his great poem:

> *The Retreat*
> Happy those early days, when I
> Shin'd in my angel-infancy!
> Before I understood this place
> Appointed for my second race,
> Or taught my soul to fancy ought
> But a white, celestial thought;
> When yet I had not walk'd above
> A mile or two from my first love,
> And looking back – at that short space –
> Could see a glimpse of His bright face;
> When on some gilded cloud, or flow'r,
> My gazing soul would dwell an hour,
> And in those weaker glories spy
> Some shadows of eternity;
> Before I taught my tongue to wound
> My conscience with a sinful sound,
> Or had the black art to dispense
> A sev'ral sin to ev'ry sense,
> But felt through all this fleshly dress
> Bright shoots of everlastingness.
>   O how I long to travel back,
> And tread again that ancient track!
> That I might once more reach that plain,
> Where first I left my glorious train;
> From whence th' enlighten'd spirit sees
> That shady City of palm-trees.
> But ah! my soul with too much stay
> Is drunk, and staggers in the way!
> Some men a forward motion love,
> But I by backward steps would move;

And when this dust falls to the urn,
In that state I came, return.

The soul comes wholly innocent and clean from its previous
life which appears to have been one of potency within the
thought of the Creator; but it is life itself, the world, which pol-
lutes, blackens the white soul, darkens the light until it floun-
ders hopelessly, leaving only fading memories of that white-
ness, that light. Even the things of nature are viewed in innocence merely as memories of that original Paradise, and are not
gazed upon or loved for their own sake; there is no sense here
that Creation itself, in its majesty, its beauty, its wonder, can
urge the soul to wallow in that Creation and thus praise its very
Maker. However the poem itself is utterly memorable, holding
as it does the sense that he simply allows his deepest emotion
here to flow forth, controlled by rhyme and its focus on the central thought. There is no doubt that the 'I' here is the poet himself at his most true, vulnerable and honest. The very perfection
of the poem in its formal glory, combined with the colouring of
loss and longing within, wholly mirrors the loss of the perfection the suffering spirit feels itself capable of, if not in the future,
then somehow in the past.

Henry Vaughan was born in 1622 to Thomas Vaughan and
Denise Morgan in Newton-upon-Usk in Breconshire, Wales. He
appears to have entered Oxford in 1638, with his twin brother
Thomas who became quite well known as a poet in his own
right and a hermetic philosopher and alchemist. In 1640
Vaughan went to study law in London for two years, a course
interrupted by the Civil War in which he briefly took the side of
the king. He is thought to have served on the Royalist side in
South Wales sometime around 1645. In 1642 he returned to
Breconshire as secretary to Judge Lloyd, and soon he was prac-
ticing medicine. He married Catherine Wise with whom he was
to have a son and three daughters. In so far as there is any influence on his work from his natural environment, Vaughan took
such a spur from the fact that he lived in south Wales where the
Celtic tribe known as the Silures, had lived and resisted the

Roman invasion of Britain. Vaughan is often referred to as 'the Silurist'.

In 1650 he published the first part of *Silex Scintillans*, his collection of religious poems. The title means 'The Sparkling Flint', and they are religious poems that touch on, as he sees it, the hardness of his own stony heart which yet, by suffering, may come to gleam and shine in God's sight. *Silex Scintillans* was reprinted in 1655 with a second, additional part. Even the Latin title indicates how removed Vaughan felt from even the beautiful Breconshire valleys in which he lived. After the death of his first wife, Vaughan married her sister Elizabeth, possibly in 1655. He had another son, and three more daughters by his second wife. He died on April 23, 1695, and was buried in Llansantffraed churchyard.

No doubt the death of his brother William, at the age of about 27, had a very strong and darkening effect on his own life and feeling. Now the world seems an even darker and emptier place:

Come, come, what do I here?
    Since he is gone
Each day is grown a dozen year,
    And each hour, one;
    Come come!
Cut off the sum,
By these soiled tears!

And another poem has it thus:

Silence, and stealth of days! 'tis now
    Since thou art gone,
Twelve hundred hours, and not a brow
    But clouds hang on.
As he that in some cave's thick damp
    Locked from the light,
Fixeth a solitary lamp,
    To brave the night ...

where Plato's image of the cave comes to mind.

Holding such a belief, Vaughan inevitably came to see the

world itself as corrupt and corrupting and this, unfortunately, has been a tenet of Christian belief for far too long, right up into our own age, though other poets have tried to refute it. The world is corrupting and man is foul and evil:

Thus thou all day a thankless weed dost dress,
And when th'hast done, a stench, or fog is all
    The odour I bequeath.
(*Unprofitableness*)

Sweet Jesu! will then; let no more
This leper haunt, and soil thy door.
(*Christ's Nativity*)

Many more instances of this can be found through the poetry of Henry Vaughan. There is, of course, the same awareness of man's state as being dust as there is in Herbert, but in Vaughan it tends more to be clay, and a putrid clay at that. This being the case, it is inevitable that poetry itself, in Vaughan's mind, be portioned only towards things beyond this earth, to faith, to God, to pleading.

And for his sake
Who died to stake
His life for mine, tune to thy will
    My heart, my verse.
(*Disorder and Frailty*)

This is followed by a poem called *Idle Verse* where Vaughan is clearly conscious of the impulse to love lyrics of his time, indeed of every time:

The purls of youthful blood, and bowels,
    Lust in the robes of love,
The idle talk of feverish souls
    Sick with a scarf, or glove.

For Vaughan then, man is a creature of vile clay, yet in that clay God has planted a seed which is his own spirit of light; this seed stirs in the darkness which it must cast off and grow high into the light. The use of the imagery of light and darkness is the most obvious one in Vaughan, almost every poem using it in some form. This leads to a longing for that last day, that final call, the great judgement when Christ's kingdom will dawn, when the night will be forever expelled and man shall at last reach fulfilment, out of vile clay into eternal light. For this Vaughan is waiting; dressed, and ready to go; and meanwhile, of course, this vile earth on which we live and move and have our being, is but a trip and a trap and a distraction:

Yet let my course, my aim, my love,
And chief acquaintance be above;
So when that day, and hour shall come
In which thy self will be the Sun,
Thou'lt find me dressed and on my way,
Watching the break of thy great day.
(The Dawning)

If mankind is made out of vile clay then it is suffering that kills off the weeds and tares that surround the growing plant. This, too, is part of the old Christian myth that is still widely held. Here we are struggling through our 'vale of tears', struggling to get across a marshy ground, the whole purpose being to reach the other side and come out as unscathed as possible. Again, the spite is for this our earth:

And since these biting frosts but kill
Some tares in me which choke or spill
That seed thou sow'st, blest be thy skill!
(Love and Discipline)

Thou art
Refining fire, oh then refine my heart,
My foul, foul heart
(Love-Sick)

Vaughan's store of images is severely limited but he has ransacked that store to such effect that the poetry works by a strange, almost unwilling and cumulative power, and a great many of those images and ideas are contained in that fine poem, The World:

The World

I saw Eternity the other night,
Like a great ring of pure and endless light,
All calm, as it was bright;
And round beneath it, Time in hours, days, years,
Driv'n by the spheres
Like a vast shadow mov'd; in which the world
And all her train were hurl'd.
The doting lover in his quaintest strain
Did there complain;
Near him, his lute, his fancy, and his flights,
Wit's sour delights,
With gloves, and knots, the silly snares of pleasure,
Yet his dear treasure
All scatter'd lay, while he his eyes did pour
Upon a flow'r.

The darksome statesman hung with weights and woe,
Like a thick midnight-fog mov'd there so slow,
He did not stay, nor go;
Condemning thoughts (like sad eclipses) scowl
Upon his soul,
And clouds of crying witnesses without
Pursued him with one shout.
Yet digg'd the mole, and lest his ways be found,
Work'd under ground,
Where he did clutch his prey; but one did see
That policy;
Churches and altars fed him; perjuries
Were gnats and flies;
It rain'd about him blood and tears, but he
Drank them as free.

The fearful miser on a heap of rust
Sate pining all his life there, did scarce trust
His own hands with the dust,
Yet would not place one piece above, but lives

In fear of thieves;
Thousands there were as frantic as himself,
And hugg'd each one his pelf;
The downright epicure plac'd heav'n in sense,
And scorn'd pretence,
While others, slipp'd into a wide excess,
Said little less;
The weaker sort slight, trivial wares enslave,
Who think them brave;
And poor despised Truth sate counting by
Their victory.

Yet some, who all this while did weep and sing,
And sing, and weep, soar'd up into the ring;
But most would use no wing.
O fools (said I) thus to prefer dark night
Before true light,
To live in grots and caves, and hate the day
Because it shews the way,
The way, which from this dead and dark abode
Leads up to God,
A way where you might tread the sun, and be
More bright than he.
But as I did their madness so discuss
One whisperd thus,
'This ring the Bridegroom did for none provide,
But for his bride.'

The politician, like the rest of us, lives in this world of darkness but Vaughan sees him as being within a deeper darkness,
digging, like the mole, and shifting his life even further off the
main course of light. The rest of us weep and sing, but sometimes find the light. The distaste for the actual world in which a
human lives was, of course, strengthened by the belief that here
we are in a shadow-world, born alienated from our true world,
that we live in darkness and misery here. All of this augmented
the poet's failure to look at nature itself; of course he may talk of

'flowers' and 'bowers', 'banks' and 'groves' but all of these fail
to touch on a real place, or real things; they remain in the realm
of abstraction and vagueness, as if nature were something to be
seen through and beyond but not rested in for its own sake:

I walked the other day
                Into a field
Where I sometimes had seen the soil to yield
                A gallant flower,
But winter now had ruffled all the bower
                And curious store
        I knew there heretofore.

'Curious store', 'gallant', 'ruffled' … such terms. 'A gallant
flower' is so vague as to be of no interest in itself, leading at once
away from actuality into Vaughan's treatise. Of course it is not
in Vaughan's interest to take a close look at the earth and relish
it; the opposite is to be the case, but as we have lived long after
the Romantic era we have been schooled to see an actual daf-
fodil with its breeze-blown loveliness, or a bank of primroses
touched into exquisite beauty by speedwell or bluebell. Yet in
the next poem there is a foretaste of what might have been possible, side by side with a blankness that is also vague; Vaughan
talks about 'some gloomy grove' but then goes on to be almost
precise:

Or those faint beams in which this hill is dress'd
After the sun's remove.

The image is accurate and moving, perhaps all because of the
use of the word 'this', the poet thinking of a precise place and
time. This poem was one of the very first to reach me when I was
still a very small child, and it came to me in this way: my grand-
mother had a fat Missal, which she brought with her to every
Mass. As she looked after us as children a great deal, I often
found myself kneeling, fidgeting, trying to pass the time, in a
pew beside her. Her Missal intrigued me, as I occasionally saw
her in tears as she poured over it. Fat in itself, it was made fatter
still by the number of Mass cards which packed it. On several of

these memorial cards were written the lines: 'They are all gone into the world of light / And I alone sit lingering here.' I wondered who 'they' were, and where this world of light was; I wondered, too, what this loneliness and lingering were all about. I would look up into the old woman's gentle face, hurt with sorrow, then gaze up at the great blaze of candles about the altar and the dim sunlight made more bright and colourful by the glazed and coloured windows. But the power of the music in the words and, of course, the strength of the statement and the imagery, brought the lines deeply into my soul where they nestled, waiting. Waiting until I came across the whole poem many, many years later and at once fell in love with the whole thing:

They Are All Gone …
They are all gone into the world of light!
   And I alone sit ling'ring here;
Their very memory is fair and bright,
    And my sad thoughts doth clear.

It glows and glitters in my cloudy breast,
   Like stars upon some gloomy grove,
Or those faint beams in which this hill is dress'd,
    After the sun's remove.

I see them walking in an air of glory,
   Whose light doth trample on my days:
My days, which are at best but dull and hoary,
    Mere glimmering and decays.

O holy Hope! and high Humility,
   High as the heavens above!
These are your walks, and you have show'd them me,
    To kindle my cold love.

Dear, beauteous Death! the jewel of the just,
   Shining nowhere, but in the dark;
What mysteries do lie beyond thy dust,
    Could man outlook that mark!

He that hath found some fledg'd bird's nest, may know
  At first sight, if the bird be flown ;
But what fair well or grove he sings in now,
    That is to him unknown.

And yet, as angels in some brighter dreams
  Call to the soul when man doth sleep,
So some strange thoughts transcend our wonted themes,
    And into glory peep.

If a star were confin'd into a tomb,
  Her captive flames must needs burn there;
But when the hand that lock'd her up, gives room,
    She'll shine through all the sphere.

O Father of eternal life, and all
  Created glories under Thee!
Resume Thy spirit from this world of thrall
    Into true liberty.

Either disperse these mists, which blot and fill
  My perspective still as they pass:
Or else remove me hence unto that hill
    Where I shall need no glass.

This is one of Vaughan's poems where the imagery of light and darkness is the most succinctly employed. Everything that is good and glorious awaits us elsewhere, not in this world! As a corollary death becomes the most desired thing; in this world is gloom and sorrow, darkness and decay, thrall and dust; in the next is brightness and joy, light and fullness, liberty and love. Yet now and again, though as we grow older in life and our 'memory' of that other world grows ever dimmer, still angels in our dreams may occasionally touch us with the glimmering of that far-off light.

The poetry of Henry Vaughan is a poetry that finds this world alien to humankind, that revels in traces of a 'memory' of a better world and longs for and moves always to find that better world. It is to be found only in death, and it is God's way and will to bring the cautious and prayerful soul to that world. Vaughan, far from being a 'mystical' poet in the true sense, is therefore the supreme example of a Christian outlook that despises the earth we move on and seeks freedom and fulfillment in the next. The troubles of the times, the wars and strife that were common, the religious bickering and the doubts about practice and ritual, all contributed, no doubt, to his approach. But it is an approach to the relationship between this world and the next that lasted far too long in the poetry of religion, and the religion of poetry. If peace is only to be found in the next world, what point is there in striving to make anything perfect in this? Yet now and again Vaughan gets the poetry right: when the poem shifts from a pleading or a complaining mode into a quick cry of personal distress or longing, when the imagery is not forced and thinned out by overuse, then his skill in verse form and rhyming lifts the work to another plane.

Peace
My soul, there is a country
    Far beyond the stars,
Where stands a wingèd sentry
    All skillful in the wars:
There, above noise and danger,
    Sweet Peace sits crown'd with smiles,
And One born in a manger
    Commands the beauteous files.
He is thy gracious Friend,
    And – O my soul awake! –
Did in pure love descend,
    To die here for thy sake.
If thou canst get but thither,
    There grows the flower of Peace,
The Rose that cannot wither,
    Thy fortress, and thy ease.
Leave then thy foolish ranges;
    For none can thee secure,
But One, who never changes,
    Thy God, thy life, thy cure.

Andrew Marvell (1621-1678)

My fruits are only flowers...

Marvell seems to have been more interested in a career in politics than in having his work published. There is very little evidence that his poetry was known in his lifetime, nor for a long time afterwards. It was T. S. Eliot's idea, three hundred years after Marvell's birth, to say he 'deserves not only the celebration proposed by that favoured borough (Hull), but a little serious reflection upon his writing'. Marvell was born in Yorkshire and his life spans the reign and fall of Charles I, the Commonwealth and the Restoration. His father was the Rev Marvell who became lecturer in Holy Trinity Church in Hull. Some days after he won a scholarship, Marvell's mother died; he left Cambridge only after his father's death, by drowning, in 1640.

Marvell travelled in Europe and in 1650 became tutor to Mary Fairfax, daughter of the retired Lord General of the parliamentary forces. He seems to have done a good deal of his writing at the Fairfax home, Nun Appleton House, examining, in a poem titled *Upon Appleton House*, the claims of public versus private life. By 1653 he was a friend of John Milton who recommended him for the post of Assistant Latin Secretary to the Council of State. Marvell now became a follower of Cromwell, tutoring his nephew at Eton. After the Restoration, Marvell seems to have returned a favour in being instrumental in saving Milton from an extended jail sentence, if not execution. In 1659 he was elected MP for Hull.

His life, then, was balanced and secure, and each move he made seems to have been taken with honest deliberation, not merely for safety's sake. He was a brief convert to Roman Catholicism. His work embodies the classical virtues of poise and elegance, though his overuse of 'does' and 'do' etc to fill out lines, somewhat detracts from their power. He was an MP up to his death, deeply engaged in political activities. His influences were Latin, his poise therefore a European poise, the simplicity of his work a studied effect. Poetry as artifice keeps the ego and poetry removed from one another and Marvell's religious work moves outside and around himself. Later generations have greatly forgotten his political activities, but remembered the graces of his finest lyrics. And how pleasing it is, particularly in *Bermudas*, to find a poet revelling in the glory of the world while singing praises to the Maker!

The Coronet

When for the thorns with which I long, too long,
    With many a piercing wound,
    My saviour's head have crowned,
I seek with garlands to redress that wrong;
    Through every garden, every mead,
I gather flowers (my fruits are only flowers),
    Dismantling all the fragrant towers
That once adorned my shepherdess's head.
And now when I have summed up all my store,
    Thinking (so I myself deceive)
    So rich a chaplet thence to weave
As never yet the king of glory wore:
    Alas, I bind the serpent old
    That, twining in his speckled breast,
    About the flowers disguised does fold,
    With wreaths of fame and interest.
Ah, foolish man, that wouldst debase with them,
And mortal glory, heaven's diadem!
But thou who only couldst the serpent tame,
Either his slippery knots at once untie,
And disentangle all his winding snare;
Or shatter too with him my curious frame,
And let these wither, so that he may die,
Though set with skill and chosen out with care:
That they, while thou on both their spoils dost tread,
May crown thy feet, that could not crown thy head.

Bermudas

Where the remote Bermudas ride
In th'ocean's bosom unespied,
From a small boat, that rowed along,
The listening winds received this song.
      'What should we do but sing his praise
That led us through the watery maze,
Unto an isle so long unknown,
And yet far kinder than our own?
Where he the huge sea-monsters wracks,
That lift the deep upon their backs,
He lands us on a grassy stage,
Safe from the storms, and prelate's rage.
He gave us this eternal spring,
Which here enamels everything,
And sends the fowl to us in care,
On daily visits through the air.
He hangs in shades the orange bright,
Like golden lamps in a green night,
And does in the pom'granates close
Jewels more rich than Ormus shows.
He makes the figs our mouths to meet,
And throws the melons at our feet,
But apples plants of such a price,
No tree could ever bear them twice.
With cedars, chosen by his hand,
From Lebanon, he stores the land,
And makes the hollow seas, that roar,
Proclaim the ambergris on shore,
He cast (of which we rather boast)
The gospel's pearl upon our coast,
And in these rocks for us did frame
A temple, where to sound his name.
Oh let our voice his praise exalt,
Till it arrive at heaven's vault:

Which thence (perhaps) rebounding, may
Echo beyond the Mexique Bay.'
  Thus sung they, in an English boat,
An holy and a cheerful note,
And all the way, to guide their chime,
With falling oars they kept the time.

Thou hast bound bones and veins in me ...

A view of the Eucharist

I associate the Feast of Corpus Christi with the month of May on Achill Island. The roads and uplands were brilliant then with the opulence of the rhododendron, great masses of purple flowers contrasting wonderfully with the liquid gold of the furze bushes, also in bloom. And here and there the glorious chestnut tree, alert and worshipful like a thousand-branched candelabrum. The church at Achill Sound was festive with bunting and we, young and old alike, were treated to a festival day; school was out, it was a public holiday, processions were taking place and the great monstrance was carried around the church and sometimes down the village road while hymns were raucous across erratically-working loudspeakers. There was a sense of generosity, of wholeness, of togetherness as if the world itself, its root, branch and foliage, were wholly given over to the celebration of this wonderful gift of bread, the Eucharist.

The documents of Vatican II describe the Eucharist as 'the source and summit of the Christian life' and when the faithful participate in it 'they offer the divine victim to God and themselves along with it'. All of which is wonderful, uplifting, and has been quite meaningless to me until recent times. When I was young, of course I accepted with delight such festive days, but they meant nothing to me in terms of sacrament or Eucharist. Our First Communion Day was such another feast; we were dressed in new suits, new shirts, new ties, we were treated as little Gods and got ourselves thoroughly sick afterwards on sweets and chocolate and lemonade. But what we were about ... well, that was never clear. We were told we were eating the Body of Christ, really present. And drinking his Blood. But we never got near the wine in the chalice. And what I remember most was the fear of taking communion in a state of sin, 'not discerning the Body of the Lord'. This was grave; it was mortal; it was terror. Where now the generosity and opulence? Where the delight and festival? It became a chore, a thing you had to do each Sunday or else, if you failed to leave your pew, you were presumed to have committed a mortal sin and could not go! 'Love bade me welcome, but my soul drew back, guilty of dust and sin.'

Now I partake of Eucharist with a wholly different attitude, one of trying to accept the abundance and opulence of a loving and never-vindictive God. After all, Jesus fed thousands of people on the side of a mountain, at the shore of a lake, so generously that from the loaves and fishes distributed to the people, the fragments gathered up afterwards would have fed many, many more. When the fishermen came in that glorious morning after the resurrection, they found Jesus with a banquet prepared for them on the shores of the lake. The disciples racing for Emmaus recognised Jesus 'in the breaking of bread', and it is clear that the Christ often and often feasted with his followers, the poor and the starving, the sinners and the outcast, as well as his own chosen disciples. All of this, and so much more in the story of Jesus' life and death, leads me to believe in Jesus' overt emphasis on love; love, love, love ... and nowhere in the events that constitute the institution of the Eucharist do I find anything about 'eating unworthily', or having to confess beforehand. It is up to us, human hesitants, to acknowledge God's abundant giving, his love, and to accept it.

This I began to feel after reading once again the great poem by George Herbert, that poem called *Love*. The dramatic movement of this poem makes clear the wholeheartedness of the invitation to dine with the Lord and the slow, reluctant response of the human heart to the generosity. There is a wonderful development as the guilt-ridden sinner gradually comes to accept the urging generosity in spite of the awareness of human frailty and sinfulness. It is simply the generosity that is so difficult for us to accept: can our God be as good as all that? Have we spent ages trying to hide this generosity from ourselves, rather emphasising our own unworthiness than accepting the giving? As I go through the canon of poetry written in English, I have found it well-nigh impossible to find poems on the Eucharist, even amongst the Catholic countries, especially in our own. I wonder why this central focus of our faith has so rarely moved a poet sufficiently to write a poem on it? Strange, unless it is the fear of unworthiness, or the slowness to allow a faith in the wholeheart-edness of that love, that hesitates the hand. Or perhaps it is the fact that poets tend more to the earthy and pagan movement of our living rather than to the regulated and doctrinaire tenets of a faith: perhaps the poet moves in the reaches of pagan marsh-lands rather than through the aisles of organised church?

If that is the case then it would be ideal to reconcile both movements. And here, I know, is where I part company with orthodoxy, yet, I hope, I do so with reason and with love urging me in this direction. Back to the idea of sinfulness: in Matthew's gospel, it is put like this: Jesus takes the bread, blesses it, breaks it and says, 'Take, eat; this is my body.' Then he takes the cup, blesses it, gives it to them and says, 'Drink from it, all of you; for this is my blood of the covenant, which is poured out for many for the forgiveness of sins.' Apart from the association of bread with his flesh and wine with his blood, it appears to me that par-taking of this sacrament in itself is 'for the forgiveness of sins'. Thus, the generosity increases. The forgiveness of sins, brought about by the overwhelming fact of Jesus giving his blood for humanity, is available to us in the Eucharist itself. In the gospel of John, where the synoptics have bread and wine, John has the washing of the feet as the central event. Now, if a sacrament, as we were taught, is the 'outward sign instituted by Christ to give grace', then this, too, is an act of forgiveness, of cleansing and of unbounded loving. The Eucharist, in its fullest form, is the link-ing of Christ's body to the bread and his blood to the wine, and all of it links to a cleansing and a forgiveness that is riotous in generosity.

The first poem I ever wrote was called *Offertory*: it was part of a Mass I was involved in where I wrote the words and Paddy

Moloney of the Chieftains wrote the music. The offertory words linked the labour of our hands with the bread, and the suffering we undergo with the wine. So we offer up all our constructive work to our God as bread, and all our suffering as wine; and it is transfigured for us by God's goodness and we take it back within us, transformed into salvific grace. Simple, and wonderful. Without dread, or fear. The whole earth involved, blessed and made holy by Eucharist.

> We offer you, Lord, in our strong, our sensitive hands
> to-day this bread:
> this plough and plod, soft coaxing, collecting,
>> the mixing and moulding, dull rumbling of trucks
>> till the crates all are named for those countless lands;
> from our proud, proud hands, O Lord, accept this bread.

> We offer you, Lord, in our soil-cracked, our swollen hands
> to-day this wine:
> this fall, this crush, the strain, the pain
>> O crumbling collapsing of flesh and the fierce
>> dizzy dash of the blood of those countless lands;
> from our weary, weary hearts, O Christ, accept this wine.

> Then give into our hands
>> your flesh
>>> to melt and merge with the soil and stones,

> and give into our hearts
>> your blood
>>> to seep through the sweat when the world
>>> groans,

> that our earth may grow through its brightest blackest parts
> a sight well pleasing to the Lord of lands.

For Gerard Manley Hopkins it was the incarnation that enriched the whole of creation, not just humankind. Let me push further. In his great poem *The Wreck of the Deutschland* Hopkins wrote:

Thou mastering me
God! givef of breath and bread;
World's strand, sway of the sea;
Lord of living and dead;
Thou hast bound bones and veins in me, fastened me flesh ...

It is a stanza that excels in bringing close a sense of God's physical, incarnate, presence, so close that 'I feel thy finger and find thee'. And further on in the same poem:

I kiss my hand
To the stars, lovely-asunder
Starlight, wafting him out of it; and
Glow, glory in thunder;
Kiss my hand to the dappled-with-damson west:
Since, tho' he is under the world's splendour and wonder,
His mystery must be instressed, stressed;
For I greet him the days I meet him, and bless when I
understand.

Once the incarnation occurred, once God wrapped himself in human flesh, then the whole of Creation partakes of incarnation; the bones and veins, the flesh and blood, of Christ are bound into the very being of the earth. Simone Weil came close to this, I feel. In an autobiographical letter she wrote: 'Christianity should contain all vocations without exception since it is catholic. In consequence the church should also. But in my eyes Christianity is catholic by right but not in fact. So many things are outside it, so many things that I love and do not want to give up, so many things that God loves, otherwise they would not be in existence ... Christianity being catholic by right but not in fact, I regard it as legitimate on my part to be a member of the church by right but not in fact, not only for a time, but for my whole life if need be.' Her insistence that the knowledge and love of Christ pervade the whole universe kept her aloof from Catholicism and suspicious of the Eucharist. But it is my belief that the Eucharist is the way that Christianity – the full following of Christ – actually pervades the universe, as its bones and veins.

'Now there are varieties of gifts, but the same Spirit; and there are varieties of services, but the same Lord; and there are varieties of activities, but it is the same God who activates all of them in everyone ... For just as the body is one and has many members, and all the members of the body, though many, are one body, so it is with Christ. For in the one Spirit we were all baptised into one body – Jews or Greeks, slaves or free – and we were all made to drink of one Spirit.' (Paul: 1 Cor 12:4-13) Weil held that the whole of creation is subject to the forward-urging power of God's love, which she terms 'necessity', the engine as it were driving the whole creation onward, through its seasons, its births, its deaths, its growth; she also sees this as 'obedience', the whole of the natural world being true to its created nature, and the radiance of this obedience, when we grow aware of it, is beauty. Weil goes further and equates this beauty with the incarnation. Humankind's closest relationship with this necessity is through suffering: 'To change the relationship between ourselves and the world in the same way as, through apprenticeship, the workman changes the relationship between himself and the tool. Getting hurt: this is the trade entering the body. May all suffering make the universe enter into the body.' The beauty of this creation, the necessary suffering undergone in its and our development, all of this gets its truth and sanctity through the incarnation, through the faith that the bones of Jesus, the veins of Jesus, have sanctified the whole of creation.

If we are all expecting, together with the whole of creation, our transformation into an eternal entity with God, then it is the Eucharist that spreads this expectation, in a gesture of cleansing and of forgiveness for our being 'guilty of dust and sin', and partaking of this sacrament takes the love of Christ and sprinkles it throughout the whole of creation. 'For the creation waits with eager longing for the revealing of the children of God; for the creation was subjected to futility, not of its own will but by the will of the one who subjected it, in hope that the creation itself will be set free from its bondage to decay and will obtain the freedom of the glory of the children of God.' (Rom 8:19-21) The world is made up, then, as we are, of the Jesus body, the Jesus veins. The whole of creation becomes the body and blood of the Son of God and thus redeemed and worthy to stand tall in the sight of God.

What it all comes down to is the immensity of the love of God, his creative power allied to his redemptive incarnation and suffering, the spreading of the bones and veins of Jesus incarnate, dead and resurrected, throughout the whole of creation and we, beyond all possible hope, are blessed with the possibility of consuming this Incarnate Love into our own being and knowing, by this sharing in love, a healing and forgiveness beyond all reason. All of this I tried to put into a poem written on the island of Gotland, Sweden, after a difficult flight from Stockholm. At midnight on the island a church bell rang out just as a summer storm was dying away. And for a moment my encounter with a poor suffering child and her father brought me back to my days serving Mass on Achill Island, the morning the priest dropped a Host and I, against all my training, picked it up and swallowed it. It was a moment of awareness of how the whole world is one with Christ through the Eucharist, how this is a cleansing and forgiving sacrament, and thus how it heals all the ills of humankind and of the universe! Oh dear, what a huge concept to try and convey in a short poem! But here goes …

Acolyte
The wildness of this night – the summer trees
ripped and letting fall their still green leaves,
and the sea battering the coast
in its huge compulsion – seems as nothing

to the midnight chime from the black tower,
reiterating that all this tumult
is but the bones of Jesus in their incarnation.
I have flown today onto the island,

our small plane tossed like jetsam on the clouds.
I watched the girl, her mutilated brain,
the father urging, how her body rocked
in unmanageable distress, her fingers

bruising a half-forgotten doll; hers, too,
the Jesus body, the Jesus bones. Once
in early morning, the congregation
was an old woman coughing against echoes

and a fly frantic against the high window;
the words the priest used were spoken out as if
they were frangible crystal: hoc – est – enim –
The Host was a sunrise out of liver-spotted hands

and I tinkled the bell with a tiny gladness;
the woman's tongue was ripped, her chin,
where I held the paten, had a growth of hairs;
her breath was fetid and the Host balanced

a moment, and fell. Acolyte I gathered
up the Deity, the perfect white of the bread
tinged where her tongue had tipped it – the
necessary God, the beautiful, the patience.

I swallowed it, taking within me
Godhead and congregation, the long obedience
of the earth's bones, and the hopeless urge
to lay my hands in solace on the world.

How Weary a Pilgrim

Anne Bradstreet: gazing at the door of the male conclave

The seventeenth century placed ever greater emphasis on intellect, as religion and science began to part company. The immediacy and simplicity of faith clearly in evidence in the poetry of Donne, Herbert, Vaughan and many more up to this time, now began to fade. By this time Catholics were beginning to search for heroic models to assert for them their sense of truth, the way Richard Crashaw had discovered Mary Magdalene. Puritanism developed out of discontent that the Elizabethan Religious Settlement was giving too much ground to 'popery', the Catholic Church. The Reformation in England had brought the church under the control of the monarchy while allowing many of its practices to continue. For some, this made doctrine unacceptably subservient to politics. The Protestants under Mary I, 'Bloody Mary', had suffered greatly and many had gone to Europe, to places like Geneva with its Calvinist ethos and Germany, with its Lutheran.

The Puritan movement was influenced by Calvinism though it sought its own church as the belief grew that existing churches had become corrupt. Puritans longed for a purifying of church practice through the rule of the Bible. Originally, Puritans constituted only the informed, committed Protestants. They objected to anything that smacked of idolatry, ornaments, ritual, organs in church, etc. It was only when the rule of the *Book of Common Prayer* was imposed throughout England that Puritanism shaped itself into a movement. Efforts by the Church of England to enforce uniformity drove them deeply into opposition. They were given the name 'Puritan' in mockery at their obsession with purifying the church.

During the English Reformation, the Church of Scotland had been born on the model of Calvinism and Presbyterianism.

When James VI of Scotland became James I of England, he placed many Puritans in powerful positions in the church. No Puritan himself, and scared of the influence they were beginning to exert, it was he who authorised the King James Bible to reinforce Anglican orthodoxy, as opposed to the Geneva Bible of the Puritans. Since Puritans took the Bible as their lead to faith and goodness, this was a most important moment.

During Charles I's reign, relations became more strained. During the Civil War, Puritans rallied to the Parliamentary forces; by now Puritanism was becoming a cultural entity, and was beginning to face great problems; Puritans were barred from many professions and as trans-Atlantic trade was growing and the Puritans were developing their own trades, they began to become wealthy. Religious tensions began to be seen as a battle between the Church of England and the Puritans. Through all of this, the hatreds, the tensions, they began to look towards America for greater freedom, for an opportunity to stand alone and build their own society. Here they could indulge in their own Bible readings, they could develop their personal morality and improve on education possibilities for all. Hierarchy in the church would be abolished and they would have no Monarch to insist on being head of their church.

Anne Bradstreet was born in Northampton, England, in 1612. Her father, Thomas Dudley, has been a leader of volunteers in the English Reformation. Anne was given a good education but was married at the age of 16 to Simon Bradstreet, nine years older than she was. He worked in the Massachusetts Bay Company and was the son of a Puritan minister. Simon and Anne emigrated to America in 1630 on the *Arabella*, one of the first ships to bring Puritans to New England to the newly-founded plantation colonies there. Many of the passengers died during the difficult crossing; the conditions on board were terrible, storms, malnutrition and general weakness taking many of them. Scurvy brought on by malnutrition claimed a great many lives.

Things did not get much easier when they arrived. Illness

held several settlers for some time, and several more of them died. Simon Bradstreet was made Chief Administrator of the colony. Now began a further struggle, with severe work required to overcome the climate, the lack of food, the primitive living conditions. For Anne, the strictness of her Puritan faith helped her; she had read a great deal at home in England and her trust in God did not fail her. Even when she began to suffer from smallpox and occasional paralysis that afflicted her joints, with her husband she formed a home and raised eight children. They eventually began to prosper and Anne's poor health, while continuing, did not cause her to lose heart.

Perhaps the greatest pain of all was the loss of the Bradstreet home in a fire and they had to start over, their standing in the Puritan community bringing them some help from their friends. Simon was away from home quite often and Anne was left very much alone. She studied and began to write.

As has been said so many times throughout human history, half of the world's population has been judged to be inferior to the other half. In our own century, the Catholic Church still insists that women have no real part in the affairs of the church. In Puritan times it was frowned upon for women to pursue their studies and if they had views on any topic, they were not encouraged to voice them. So she kept her poetry a secret, shared only with her family and a very close circle of friends.

But someone had copied out Anne's work, without her knowing, and had it published in England without her permission. This was titled *The Tenth Muse Lately Sprung Up in America, By a Gentlewoman of Those Parts*, published in 1650. We are left to hope in her secret satisfaction at the publication and the decent reception the poems received. She continued to write and developed a *Prologue* which, it is to be hoped, is peppered with irony:

> I am obnoxious to each carping tongue
> Who says my hand a needle better fits.
> A Poet's Pen all scorn I should thus wrong,
> For such despite they cast on female wits.

If what I do prove well, it won't advance,
They'll say it's stol'n, or else it was by chance.
...

Let Greeks be Greeks, and Women what they are.
Men have precedency and still excel;
It is but vain unjustly to wage war.
Men can do best, and Women know it well.
Preeminence in all and each is yours;
Yet grant some small acknowledgement of ours.

That last line is telling but the tone throughout is just sufficiently ironic, sufficiently proud, to allow this intelligent and
cautious woman a place higher than she is allowed to claim for
herself.

She had suffered illness all her life and now contracted tuber-
culosis; around the same time her daughter Dorothy died.
Through all of this there is no doubt that the strength of her faith
kept her sanity intact, and the fact that she continued with her
verses shows how important that particular revolt was in her
life. She herself died in Andover, Massachusetts, at the age 60.

Anne Bradstreet's work in poetry was the first by a woman to
be published in America. Her themes remain simple and constant: her faith, the love she had for her husband and family, her
hopes of a better world beyond this. Her forms, too, are simple
and repeated, basically the rhyming couplet, but within these
limitations the lines move with a fluidity and naturalness of
which she was proud. Aware of the Puritan demands and stric-
tures, aware, too, that the writing of poetry by a woman, even
the attempt at using her own mind and developing her own
thoughts, would have been regarded as sinful, Anne made a
concession to these demands by keeping the form clear and
direct, avoiding any excess of imagery or display of technique.
Her great and undoubted achievement is to have written so fine
a body of work within these manifold boundaries and restric-
tions.

Her modest (perhaps) view of her own work and her slight

effort to make amends for seeing it in book form, drew this poem from her:

The Author To Her Book
Thou ill-formed offspring of my feeble brain,
Who after birth did'st by my side remain,
Till snatched from thence by friends, less wise than true,
Who thee abroad exposed to public view,
Made thee in rags, halting to th' press to trudge,
Where errors were not lessened (all may judge).
At thy return my blushing was not small,
My rambling brat (in print) should mother call.
I cast thee by as one unfit for light,
Thy visage was so irksome in my sight,
Yet being mine own, at length affection would
Thy blemishes amend, if so I could.
I washed thy face, but more defects I saw,
And rubbing off a spot, still made a flaw.
I stretched thy joints to make thee even feet,
Yet still thou run'st more hobbling than is meet.
In better dress to trim thee was my mind,
But nought save home-spun cloth, i' th' house I find.
In this array, 'mongst vulgars may'st thou roam.
In critic's hands, beware thou dost not come,
And take thy way where yet thou art not known.
If for thy father asked, say, thou hadst none;
And for thy mother, she alas is poor,
Which caused her thus to send thee out of door

Firstly she knew, and we know, that her brain was far from 'feeble'. Someone, (she knows who), brought them in 'rags' to England and nobody there corrected them. It is hard to believe that her 'friend' copied the poems without her knowledge, or that he would have published them without some form of consent from Anne herself. She admits that eventually she allowed the book into her life, corrected and amended things in the poems, and continued to write. Her concession to a knowledge of form limits her to 'home-spun cloth', a form natural to her, avoiding false show and pride. She is aware of the danger of critics and the final line, given all that has happened to allow the poems into print, is indeed quite bristling with irony.

And what of the poems, then? And in our age, our thrust towards finally winning a place for women as equal in everything, including priesthood and hierarchy in the Catholic Church, does Anne Bradstreet speak still? The irony which we have witnessed, certainly still appeals.

Before the Birth of One of Her Children
All things within this fading world hath end,
Adversity doth still our joys attend;
No ties so strong, no friends so dear and sweet,
But with death's parting blow are sure to meet.
The sentence past is most irrevocable,
A common thing, yet oh, inevitable.
How soon, my Dear, death may my steps attend,
How soon't may be thy lot to lose thy friend,
We both are ignorant, yet love bids me
These farewell lines to recommend to thee,
That when the knot's untied that made us one,
I may seem thine, who in effect am none.
And if I see not half my days that's due,
What nature would, God grant to yours and you;
The many faults that well you know I have
Let be interred in my oblivious grave;
If any worth or virtue were in me,
Let that live freshly in thy memory
And when thou feel'st no grief, as I no harms,
Yet love thy dead, who long lay in thine arms,
And when thy loss shall be repaid with gains
Look to my little babes, my dear remains.
And if thou love thyself, or loved'st me,
These O protect from stepdame's injury.
And if chance to thine eyes shall bring this verse,
With some sad sighs honor my absent hearse;

And kiss this paper for thy dear love's sake,
Who with salt tears this last farewell did take.

Life was not easy in those times and Anne knew it; this poem
she wrote as a kind of will and testament to her husband. It is a
poem she secreted somewhere but again there is no doubt she
knew he would come across it at some stage. 'And if chance to
thine eyes shall bring this verse ...' This is a poem that otherwise
appears to be without guile, a love poem genuinely filled with
faith and a sense of sorrow, but brimming over with love both
for her husband and her children. Her one dread is that a 'stepdame' might take over when she herself is gone and she believes
such a person would surely harm her children. There is an
innocence in this that contrasts with the quiet guile we sense in
the other poems. If, then, there is a quiet battle going on in this
woman's breast between her desire, her need, to express herself
and her hopes, faith and loves in verse, and her awareness that
that very faith is disposed to censure her for that activity, she
grows even more aware that there is a quiet battle between her
faith and the world she lives in. The battle, in her mind, takes the
form of the urges of the flesh faced with the needs of the spirit.
Her poem *The Flesh and the Spirit* expresses this in a traditional
way; it is indeed a sort of homily yet the very beginning of the
poem, when the I stands alone 'in a secret place', she reveals that
she was close to tears over the clash between desire and faith.
The river, the 'Lacrim flood', is a river of tears, never far from
the Puritan's idea of human living. She pursues the argument
between flesh and spirit, but of course the conclusion is never in
doubt; of the two sisters it will be spirit who will win the day.

The Flesh and the Spirit
In secret place where once I stood
Close by the Banks of Lacrim flood,
I heard two sisters reason on
Things that are past and things to come.

Perhaps it is my own misguided sense of flesh and spirit that detects, in the complaints thrown at Spirit by Flesh, the same sarcasm already detected in other poems? Flesh asks:

Dost dream of things beyond the Moon
And dost thou hope to dwell there soon?
Hast treasures there laid up in store
That all in th' world thou count'st but poor?

When Spirit replies she begins by begging that such thoughts, of wealth, ease, fame, honour, cease to trouble her mind. Her mind, then, has been troubled, unsettled by such thoughts.

Be still, thou unregenerate part,
Disturb no more my settled heart ...
Thou speak'st me fair but hat'st me sore.
Thy flatt'ring shews I'll trust no more.
How oft thy slave hast thou me made
When I believ'd what thou hast said
And never had more cause of woe
Than when I did what thou bad'st do.
I'll stop mine ears at these thy charms
And count them for my deadly harms.

The delights of the next world are described in fairly conventional terms, culled from the Bible, and most richly from the Book of Revelations. Again the smooth and gracious couplets hold the reader and move with a quietly convinced and convincing music. Yet the restlessness of soul is there, the urge of the Flesh is strong. There is another beautiful poem, short and very carefully wrought, that touches on this restlessness. Perhaps even the most saintly of persons has doubts, but for a Puritan in those early days to express such doubts was a most dangerous thing to do, particularly when we are not convinced that the verses were put away with complete care!

By Night when Others Soundly Slept
By night when others soundly slept
And hath at once both ease and Rest,

My waking eyes were open kept
And so to lie I found it best.

I sought him whom my Soul did Love,
With tears I sought him earnestly.
He bow'd his ear down from Above.
In vain I did not seek or cry.

My hungry Soul he fill'd with Good;
He in his Bottle put my tears,
My smarting wounds washed in his blood,
And banished thence my Doubts and fears.

What to my Saviour shall I give
Who freely hath done this for me?
I'll serve him here whilst I shall live
And Love him to Eternity

The immediacy of the scene, the sleeplessness, the tears and
doubts, all are wonderfully clearly expressed. If we detect little
more than a forcing of the will in the last stanza, then that again
is not to detract from Anne's faith because faith is a matter of
will; what is special here is that it is at all written down. Most of
her poetry moves through matters domestic, her life being filled
with incident but those incidents bearing on family, births, sufferings, love, death and accident. But within this domesticity remain still those hints and suggestions, those short, snappy efforts
towards flight that leave the verses tingling in the reader's mind.

In Reference to her Children
I had eight birds hatched in one nest,
Four Cocks were there, and Hens the rest.
I nursed them up with pain and care,
No cost nor labour did I spare
Till at the last they felt their wing,
Mounted the Trees and learned to sing.
Chief of the Brood then took his flight
To Regions far and left me quite.

My mournful chirps I after send
Till he return, or I do end.
Leave not thy nest, thy Dame and Sire,
Fly back and sing amidst this Quire.
My second bird did take her flight
And with her mate flew out of sight.
Southward they both their course did bend,
And Seasons twain they there did spend,
Till after blown by Southern gales
They Northward steered with filled sails.
A prettier bird was no where seen,
Along the Beach, among the treen.
I have a third of colour white
On whom I plac'd no small delight,
Coupled with mate loving and true,
Hath also bid her Dame adieu.
And where Aurora first appears,
She now hath perched to spend her years.
One to the Academy flew
To chat among that learned crew.
Ambition moves still in his breast
That he might chant above the rest,
Striving for more than to do well,
That nightingales he might excell.
My fifth, whose down is yet scarce gone,
Is 'mongst the shrubs and bushes flown
And as his wings increase in strength
On higher boughs he'll perch at length.
My other three still with me nest
Until they're grown, then as the rest,
Or here or there, they'll take their flight,
As is ordained, so shall they light.
If birds could weep, then would my tears
Let others know what are my fears
Lest this my brood some harm should catch
And be surpris'd for want of watch

Whilst pecking corn and void of care
They fall un'wares in Fowler's snare;
Or whilst on trees they sit and sing
Some untoward boy at them do fling,
Or whilst allured with bell and glass
The net be spread and caught, alas;
Or lest by Lime-twigs they be foiled;
Or by some greedy hawks be spoiled.
O would, my young, ye saw my breast
And knew what thoughts there sadly rest.
Great was my pain when I you bred,
Great was my care when I you fed.
Long did I keep you soft and warm
And with my wings kept off all harm.
My cares are more, and fears, than ever,
My throbs such now as 'fore were never.
Alas, my birds, you wisdom want
Of perils you are ignorant.
Oft times in grass, on trees, in flight,
Sore accidents on you may light.
O to your safety have an eye,
So happy may you live and die.
Mean while, my days in tunes I'll spend
Till my weak lays with me shall end.
In shady woods I'll sit and sing
And things that past, to mind I'll bring.
Once young and pleasant, as are you,
But former toys (no joys) adieu!
My age I will not once lament
But sing, my time so near is spent,
And from the top bough take my flight
Into a country beyond sight
Where old ones instantly grow young
And there with seraphims set song.
No seasons cold, nor storms they see
But spring lasts to eternity.

When each of you shall in your nest
Among your young ones take your rest,
In chirping languages oft them tell
You had a Dame that loved you well,
That did what could be done for young
And nursed you up till you were strong
And 'fore she once would let you fly
She shewed you joy and misery,
Taught what was good, and what was ill,
What would save life, and what would kill.
Thus gone, amongst you I may live,
And dead, yet speak and counsel give.
Farewell, my birds, farewell, adieu,
I happy am, if well with you.

This poem lifts into flight because of Anne Bradstreet's control over the couplet and because of the central bird and chick imagery sustained right to the very end. The couplets, in their onward slow and yet definite impetus, convey in themselves a certain tenderness and sadness together, and the metaphorical unity also insists on the fact that here is a singer, the Dame who is writing verses, and these 'harmless' verses will serve as presence even after her death.

The great and dramatic event in the lives of the Bradstreets, apart from the illnesses, the death of her daughter, the absences of her husband, was the complete destruction of the home by fire. If it is, in our time, felt too easy that suffering and loss be accepted in the light of the faith in a next life, it must always be remembered that here we have a Puritan speaking, and speaking in an age when the slightest doubt would have seemed a sin, when the smallest complaint against the workings of God would be a terrible failure of spirit. And Anne Bradstreet, in spite of the fact that she was surreptitiously writing her verses, coped with most of her many sufferings by referring everything to a higher Power and by accepting that worldly goods are but dross and the real gold is waiting in heaven.

Raise up thy thoughts above the sky
That dunghill mists away may fly.

That familiar imagery of all things earthly falling into dust
appears in this poem; yet there is a strong effusion of her sense
of loss, she holds to faith but of course faith is not strong enough
to quell completely all earthly desires. Honesty and self-knowledge shine through this carefully orchestrated poem in praise of
a chastising God. The final couplets are a gesture of throwing
her hands in the air and finally yielding to the inevitable; they
do not have the sense of a complete and wholly unquestioning
faith about them. Here, too, she displays how she can use her
rhyming couplets to tell a story effectively; the running along of
the couplets towards those final lines effectively bring us along
with them, though, because of that slight ambivalence always
there in the poetry, we are not entirely convinced that she is entirely convinced. And this, in a poet of this excellence, is not an
accident.

Verses upon the Burning of our House
In silent night when rest I took,
For sorrow near I did not look,
I wakened was with thundering noise
And piteous shrieks of dreadful voice.
That fearful sound of 'fire' and 'fire,'
Let no man know is my Desire.
I starting up, the light did spy,
And to my God my heart did cry
To straighten me in my Distress
And not to leave me succourless.
Then coming out, behold a space
The flames consume my dwelling place.
And when I could no longer look,
I blessed his grace that gave and took,
That laid my goods now in the dust.
Yea, so it was, and so 'twas just.

It was his own; it was not mine.
Far be it that I should repine,
He might of all justly bereft
But yet sufficient for us left.
When by the Ruins oft I past
My sorrowing eyes aside did cast
And here and there the places spy
Where oft I sate and long did lie.
Here stood that Trunk, and there that chest,
There lay that store I counted best,
My pleasant things in ashes lie
And them behold no more shall I.
Under the roof no guest shall sit,
Nor at thy Table eat a bit.
No pleasant talk shall 'ere be told
Nor things recounted done of old.
No Candle 'ere shall shine in Thee,
Nor bridegroom's voice 'ere heard shall be.
In silence ever shalt thou lie.
Adieu, Adieu, All's Vanity.
Then straight I 'gin my heart to chide:
And did thy wealth on earth abide,
Didst fix thy hope on mouldring dust,
The arm of flesh didst make thy trust?
Raise up thy thoughts above the sky
That dunghill mists away may fly.
Thou hast a house on high erect
Framed by that mighty Architect,
With glory richly furnished
Stands permanent, though this be fled.
It's purchasèd and paid for too
By him who hath enough to do.
A price so vast as is unknown,
Yet by his gift is made thine own.
There's wealth enough; I need no more.
Farewell, my pelf; farewell, my store.

The world no longer let me love;
My hope and Treasure lies above

This last line provided Mistress Bradstreet with the theme
that would certainly show to any curious or denouncing eyes
that she as a poet was merely wishing to instruct her children in
the highest ways of the world. A poem like *The Vanity of All
Worldly Things* is a hugely competent work in couplets, exemplary in every way, and ultimately dull. Yet there are poems
where the intensity of her affection, her love, is for her husband.
I am not convinced that a poem so purely framed, so strong with
the sentiment of human loving, would have gone down so well
among the saints.

To my Dear and Loving Husband
If ever two were one, then surely we.
If ever man were loved by wife, then thee.
If ever wife was happy in a man,
Compare with me, ye women, if you can.
I prize thy love more than whole Mines of gold
Or all the riches that the East doth hold.
My love is such that Rivers cannot quench,
Nor ought but love from thee give recompense.
Thy love is such I can no way repay.
The heavens reward thee manifold, I pray.
Then while we live, in love let's so persever
That when we live no more, we may live ever.

Let Sorrow Find a Way

William Cowper and John Clare

William Cowper (1731-1800) was the fourth child of Rev John Cowper, Chaplain to George II. He was not yet six when his older siblings died and his mother Anne died in childbirth when his brother John was born. He was severely bullied for some two years in school. He was called to the Bar in 1754 and founded a 'Nonsense Club', a society in Westminster of men who dined together and wrote ballads. Already, as he worked to have himself qualified, he was suffering from depression and made attempts at suicide. Eventually he was placed in an Asylum in St Albans and greatly improved under the care of one Dr Cotton, a poet and evangelical. When he left the asylum he became dependent on relatives and friends for financial support. His brother John was in Cambridge and William moved to Huntingdon to be near him. Here he became friends with one William Unwin who introduced him to his parents, the Rev Morley Unwin and his wife, Mary. Cowper lodged with the family and stayed close to them for over twenty years.

At this time he found some peace and comfort in gardening and in his friendship with the family but after about a year and a half the Rev Unwin was killed in a riding accident and Mary wished to leave Huntingdon to find a town where an evangelical minister would be pastor. She discovered Olney where the Rev John Newton was curate and in 1768 Cowper moved to Olney with the Unwin family. Newton was a former captain of a slaveship and he and his wife Mary grew close to William Cowper and Mary Unwin.

Cowper wrote: 'Olney is a populous place, inhabited chiefly by the half starved and ragged of the Earth.' It was an old lace town where women spent most of the day making lace and gangs of children were left to roam through the streets. Newton helped distribute alms to the poor of Olney and Cowper helped him in this charitable work.

Then in 1769 Mary Unwin became seriously ill; she had been an intelligent and sympathetic companion to Cowper; she was very religious and William had come to regard her as a mother figure. She recovered and William appears to have taken the more seriously to writing his hymns in order to further the good work of Newton's sermons. *Olney Hymns* were published in 1779 and included the hymn *Amazing Grace*, written by Newton. In 1779 Mary and William became engaged.

It was at this time that Cowper's mental health deteriorated again. He appears to have been deeply worried about this engagement and felt that God had rejected him. He made another suicide attempt, was again treated by Dr Cotton and recovered. However, this breakdown led to the breaking off of his engagement. He also wrote many letters at this time, as they helped to ease his mind, letters full of news of his garden, his greenhouse, his experiments with pineapples and melons and cucumbers, and his joy in looking after hares. Late in 1779 Newton left Olney to become rector of a parish in London. He continued to correspond with Cowper. Conditions in Olney became worse and Cowper grew ever more aware of the suffering and starvation of the population. He was now writing more poetry than hymns and published a volume of poems in 1782. He wrote his major poem *The Task* about this time, a poem Robert Burns spoke of as 'the religion of God and Nature: the religion that exults, that ennobles man'.

Cowper, together with Mary Unwin, moved to a village some two miles from Olney. He began to work on a translation of Homer, which was published in 1791 and brought him in some hefty royalties. During this time Mary's health suffered and Cowper helped to nurse her. He had been awarded a pension of £300 per annum but the strain of looking after Mary also brought Cowper to the edge. In 1796 he moved with Mary to Norfolk. In December of that year, Mary died. Cowper lived on in poor mental health and he died in April 1800.

Cowper's life, then, was a strange one, hovering between wellbeing and insanity, on the edge of great friendship but never moving over into love and marriage. His living among the poor and suffering, as well as his own physical and mental distress, led him to view the world as a dark and difficult place and he filled his own mind with doubts and scruples.

The Contrite Heart
The Lord will happiness divine
    On contrite hearts bestow;
Then tell me, gracious God, is mine
    A contrite heart, or no?

I hear, but seem to hear in vain,
    Insensible as steel;
If ought is felt, 'tis only pain,
    To find I cannot feel.

I sometimes think myself inclined
    To love thee, if I could;
But often feel another mind,
    Averse to all that's good.

My best desires are faint and few,
    I fain would strive for more;
But when I cry, 'My strength renew!'
    Seem weaker than before.

Thy saints are comforted I know,
    And love thy house of prayer;
I therefore go where others go,
    But find no comfort there.

O make this heart rejoice, or ache;
    Decide this doubt for me;
And if it be not broken, break –
    And heal it if it be.

How does one know if one's heart is 'contrite'? A question like that, asked with such intensity, indicates a troubled spirit.

Apart from the lifelong sense of loss after the death of his mother, Cowper never found himself fully at ease in this world. In the company of the Rev Unwin and later of the Rev Newton, he found some peace in his belief in God. But this, too, proved to be uncertain and he was unable to contain this uncertainty. The hymns he wrote, carefully modulated and ordered to suit their occasion, bristle with a sense of the personality of the writer and therefore surpass the condition of so many bland and soul-wearying hymns. But though Cowper tried hard to keep these hymns in check, the same doubts and hesitancies rumble through. There is always a sense of sinfulness, though Cowper's life was lived in the deepest quietness and safety; there is, too, a sense that the early peace and happiness he had found in his first discovery of God, has been lost because of sin. Here is none of Herbert's acceptance of his own sinfulness because he knows it will be overcome by God's love; nor is there here any notion of the will and determination of a John Donne, nor the all-too-much reaching out of Henry Vaughan. Here, in hymns written to be sung by a rural congregation, is hesitation, doubt and fear.

Walking With God
Oh! for a closer walk with God,
    A calm and heavenly frame;
A light to shine upon the road
    That leads me to the Lamb!

Where is the blessedness I knew
    When first I saw the Lord?
Where is the soul-refreshing view
    Of Jesus, and his word?

What peaceful hours I once enjoyed
    How sweet their memory still!
But they have left an aching void,
    The world can never fill.

Return, O holy Dove, return,
  Sweet messenger of rest;
I hate the sins that made thee mourn,
  And drove thee from my breast.

The dearest idol I have known,
  Whate'er that idol be;
Help me to tear it from thy throne,
  And worship only thee.

So shall my walk be close with God,
  Calm and serene my frame;
So purer light shall mark the road
  That leads me to the Lamb.

This emphasis on sin and doubt, and on melancholy, is distressing. Indeed, and in spite of his real faith in God, Cowper battled all his life with depression and eventually, scared of giving himself to human loving, fell at last into despair and hopelessness. In a letter to Newton he said: 'Loaded as my life is with despair, I have no such comfort as would result from a supposed probability of better things to come, were it once ended ... You will tell me that this cold gloom will be succeeded by a cheerful spring, and endeavour to encourage me to hope for a spiritual change resembling it – but it will be lost labour. Nature revives again; but a soul once slain lives no more ... My friends ... think it necessary to the existence of divine truth, that he who once had possession of it should never finally lose it. I admit the solidity of this reasoning in every case but my own. And why not in my own? ... I forestall the answer: – God's ways are mysterious, and He giveth no account of His matters: – an answer that would serve my purpose as well as theirs that use it. There is a mystery in my destruction, and in time it shall be explained.'

This sense that he alone is the one to lose God's care and attention is one common to those who suffer the deepest depression. He has sinned and although he repents he holds to a God that will not make clear, through faith, that repentance is enough. This God he believes in is mysterious and beyond mys-

terious; therefore hope is vague and useless. There is one great
poem of hope when this despair is forthrightly and willfully set
aside. From the rest of the work this poem stands out as a moment of true hope and real faith but there is to it almost too
much statement, too much determination that things will be so,
too much insisting.

Light Shining Out of Darkness
God moves in a mysterious way,
  His wonders to perform;
He plants his footsteps in the sea,
  And rides upon the storm.

Deep in unfathomable mines
  Of never failing skill,
He treasures up his bright designs,
  And works his sovereign will.

Ye fearful saints, fresh courage take,
  The clouds ye so much dread
Are big with mercy, and shall break
  In blessings on your head.

Judge not the Lord by feeble sense,
  But trust him for his grace;
Behind a frowning providence,
  He hides a smiling face.

His purposes will ripen fast,
  Unfolding ev'ry hour;
The bud may have a bitter taste,
  But sweet will be the flow'r.

Blind unbelief is sure to err,
  And scan his work in vain;
God is his own interpreter,
  And he will make it plain.

And so it goes on, poem after poem, filled with self-doubt,
with a willing himself into faith and some form of hope.

Generally, church hymns are dull stuff, offering repeated clichés of faith and hope and plea; it is thanks to the doubts and miseries of William Cowper's personal suffering that we have hymns that surpass such dry exercises.

Peace After a Storm
When darkness long has veiled my mind,
And smiling day once more appears;
Then, my Redeemer, then I find
The folly of my doubts and fears.

Straight I upbraid my wand'ring heart,
And blush that I should ever be
Thus prone to act so base a part,
Or harbour one hard thought of thee!

Oh! let me then at length be taught
What I am still so slow to learn;
That God is love, and changes not,
Nor knows the shadow of a turn.

Sweet truth, and easy to repeat!
But when my faith is sharply tried,
I find myself a learner yet,
Unskilful, weak, and apt to slide.

But, O my Lord, one look from thee
Subdues the disobedient will;
Drives doubt and discontent away,
And thy rebellious worm is still.

Thou art as ready to forgive,
As I am ready to repine;
Thou, therefore, all the praise receive;
Be shame and self-abhorrence mine.

There is his great long poem *The Task*, written between 1783 and 1784; of it he wrote: 'The history of the following production is briefly this: – A lady, fond of blank verse, demanded a poem of that kind from the author, and gave him the SOFA for a subject. He obeyed; and having much leisure, connected another subject with it: and, pursuing the train of thought to which his situation and turn of mind led him, brought forth at length, instead of the trifle which he at first intended, a serious affair – a Volume!' Leisure he had aplenty! Women around him took care of him! And when he let fly with this piece all his pent-up thoughts and feelings came flooding out. Freed from the constraints of the hymn, freed from the restraints of sacred subjects, Cowper developed a finely flowing blank verse that would later urge Wordsworth to follow the same path, and he allowed his natural love for solitude and nature to take him over. *The Task* is the first fine poem in English that takes nature seriously, for itself, naming the plants, trees, animals, naming the joy and peace that nature brings; it is the poem that best anticipates the Romantic imagination. And all of this from a poet whose life was mired in depression, doubt and a fierce religiosity.

> Mighty winds,
> That sweep the skirt of some far-spreading wood
> Of ancient growth, make music not unlike
> The dash of ocean on his winding shore,
> And lull the spirit while they fill the mind,
> Unnumbered branches waving in the blast,
> And all their leaves fast flutt'ring, all at once.

The poem swings along with extraordinary verve and energy, shifting from subject to subject, offering advice and suggestion, urging an end to slavery and a shift from the unnatural ambience of towns:

> Strange! there should be found
> Who self-imprison'd in their proud saloons,
> Renounce the odours of the open field
> For the unscented fictions of the loom;
> Who satisfied with only pencil'd scenes,
> Prefer to the performance of a God
> Th'inferior wonders of an artist's hand.
> Lovely indeed the mimic works of art,
> But Nature's works far lovelier.

This is a poetry liberated from the chains of form itself, only the natural metre of the English language, the iambic pentameter, offering easy ditches to the side. There is a sense in the poem that the author feels wholly free wandering among the scenes, sounds, scents that he loves because here he is free from any responsibility save to capture his own thoughts and reactions. Here he is away from the demanding presence of others and in the poetry that same freedom – no John Newton or other parson to urge hymn or scruple – is given its power and so he writes:

Oh for a lodge in some vast wilderness,
Some boundless contiguity of shade,
Where rumour of oppression and deceit,
Of unsuccessful or successful war
Might never reach me more. My ear is pain'd,
My soul is sick with ev'ry day's report
Of wrong and outrage with which earth is fill'd.

While in this mood Cowper found that he could speak to his own soul more gently about the love of Christ; in a delightful passage in this long poem all sense of scruple is gone, all doubt of self, all deep and soul-destructive misery has given way. In this lack of constraint the imagery, too, takes on a more natural and deeply memorable force and then he feels that the Christ comes far more close to him than in the chains of everyday living:

I was a stricken deer, that left the herd
Long since; with many an arrow deep infixt
My panting side was charg'd, when I withdrew
To seek a tranquil death in distant shades.
There was I found by one who had himself
Been hurt by th' archers. In his side he bore,
And in his hands and feet, the cruel scars.
With gentle force soliciting the darts,
He drew them forth, and heal'd, and bade me live.
Since then, with few associates, in remote

And silent woods I wander, far from those
My former partners of the peopled scene;
With few associates, and not wishing more.

In spite of this poem, and in spite of all the liberty he allowed
himself here, the pains of doubt and despair continued to trouble him. Some form of clinical depression, we would have no
hesitation in saying now, dogged his years. He told his doctor in
early 1800: 'I feel unutterable despair.' His early years had witnessed many deaths among his brothers and sisters, and his
mother's death must have left a lasting sense of sadness in his
life.

My mother! when I learned that thou wast dead,
Say, wast thou conscious of the tears I shed?
Hovered thy spirit o'er thy sorrowing son,
Wretch even then, life's journey just begun?

I heard the bell tolled on thy burial day,
I saw the hearses that bore thee slow away,
And turning from my nursery window, drew
A long, long sigh, and wept a last adieu!

Mrs Unwin became a mother substitute, no doubt, and
Cowper was always afraid of entering into any firm relationship, often confusing the women who watched over him and
cared for him. Cowper saw himself as a great sinner, a repro-
bate, and felt that, in spite of occasional moments of religious
contentment and hope, he was doomed to hell. That long period
of peace and contentment, as well as the free flow of his verses
while writing *The Task*, was about the only time in this sad life
when God was gently present to his easeful soul. The best of the
rest of the poetry still remains in the urgent crying of this creature to his Creator, a plea that God control his will, his strength,
his hope, his despair. And for this we are grateful, for a handful
of hymns that far surpass the normal and the dull:

Temptation
The billows swell, the winds are high,
Clouds overcast my wintry sky;
Out of the depths to thee I call,
My fears are great, my strength is small.

O Lord, the pilot's part perform,
And guard and guide me through the storm;
Defend me from each threatening ill,
Control the waves – say, 'Peace! be still!'

Amidst the roaring of the sea,
My soul still hangs her hope on thee;
Thy constant love, thy faithful care,
Is all that saves me from despair.

Dangers of ev'ry shape and name
Attend the followers of the Lamb,
Who leave the world's deceitful shore,
And leave it to return no more.

Tho' tempest-toss'd and half a wreck,
My Saviour thro' the floods I seek;
Let neither winds nor stormy main,
Force back my shatter'd bark again.

The long, hard struggle that William Cowper went through is something other than that of John Clare, born in the village of Helpstone, Northamptonshire, in 1793. He was born into the home of an agricultural labourer and had little or no formal education. He read and loved James Thompson's *Seasons* and started to write his own verses, publishing his first book and paying for it himself. It did not do well but John Taylor, the publisher of Keats, read and liked it and in 1820 published Clare's *Poems Descriptive of Rural Life*. This brought Clare into a society that was utterly alien to his private, agricultural background, an elite society where he felt himself an outsider. He was very poor, finding a small income by doing odd jobs, as lime-burner, gardener, haymaker, jack-of-all-trades. As he moved and worked in the fields he composed his poems and became, for the literary society of London, a fine curiosity. His publishers began to earn a good deal of money from Clare's work but Clare himself made little.

One of the great delights of Clare's work is the occasional use of Northamptonshire dialect, as in the lines 'the sailing puddock's shrill peelew'. This kind of thing, together with his accurate and loving description of the countryside about him, added to the sense of curiosity and weirdness so beloved of the literary hangers-on. And of course, John Clare was in love. He had married and was trying to support his wife and seven children. His strange fame called him away from home too often; he visited London where he met writers like Hazlitt, De Quincey, Coleridge, who liked him but could not make him a permanent part of their company. His fellow villagers began to become suspicious of his fame and his contacts and Clare felt ever more and more sidelined in life. But there was Mary, Mary Joyce: daughter of a farmer who lived nearby, a very beautiful young woman who appears to have reciprocated the young John Clare's affections. They met frequently but their meetings were stolen, without the knowledge of Mary's father. When eventually the farmer did find out he strictly forbade any further meetings. Clare wrote much of his love poetry to Mary, although his actual wife, 'Patty', was the subject of his admitted love poems. Mary Joyce remained always in Clare's mind the ideal of true love and real beauty and later, when his mind became disturbed, it was Mary who came to visit him in his suffering brain, although by then she was long dead.

Clare's liking for strong drink also began to cause further troubles. He spent most of his income on food for his family, often depriving himself and yet drinking to excess. He suffered from occasional 'swoonings', a kind of panic attack. By 1823 a heavy depression began to settle on him and he never recovered fully. He was eventually admitted to an insane asylum where he became, at once, more delusional. He spent some four years there before he discharged himself and walked home; he had to walk over 80 miles, which took him well over three days and he lived for that period on grass and herbs he found by the road-side. Later in that same year, 1841, he was certified as insane and committed to the Northampton Asylum. There he stayed until his death in 1864. Twenty-three years! Whatever the nature of his sorry disorder, it is clear that Clare really suffered greatly. His mental confusions were serious and hurtful, as he lost a sense of who he was and what life was about. And yet, when he carries his self-awareness and his simplicity of thought and language into an honest appraisal of life, his poetry touches deeply. Underneath his unsophisticated forms, though rarely expressed, is a strong and unshaken sense of God's existence as the ultimate arbiter of truth, of the certainty that his frustrated love and his frustrated dreams will at last be fulfilled. He placed himself wholly in God's care.

> And he who studies nature's volume through
> And reads it with a pure unselfish mind
> Will find God's power all round in every view
> As one bright vision of the almighty mind
> His eyes are open though the world is blind
> No ill from him creation's works deform
> The high and lofty one is great and kind
> Evil may cause the blight and crushing storm
> His is the sunny glory and the calm

For John Clare, self-knowledge and humility held together whatever strands of sanity he was left with. And it is a self-knowledge in touch with and sustained by God, not the God of theologians, of pastors or mystics, but the God of the country-side that Clare loved and longed to live in.

The Peasant Poet
> He loved the brook's soft sound
> The swallow swimming by
> He loved the daisy-covered ground
> The cloud-bedappled sky
> To him the dismal storm appeared

The very voice of God
And where the Evening rock was reared
Stood Moses with his rod
And every thing his eyes surveyed
The insects i' the brake
Were creatures God almighty made
He loved them for his sake
A silent man in life's affairs
A thinker from a Boy
A Peasant in his daily cares –
The Poet in his joy

The movement of this poem is natural and gentle, the rhymes are easy and full, the whole has a sense of peace to it that was gained perhaps only in John Clare's poems, and not in his sorry life. And what an honest line: *A silent man in life's affairs* ... and what an honest poem. But his self-awareness goes deeper than this in another poem:

I Am
I am – yet what I am, none cares or knows;
   My friends forsake me like a memory lost:
I am the self-consumer of my woes –
   They rise and vanish in oblivion's host
Like shadows in love-frenzied stifled throes
   And yet I am, and live – like vapours tossed

Into the nothingness of scorn and noise,
   Into the living sea of waking dreams,
Where there is neither sense of life or joys,
   But the vast shipwreck of my life's esteems;
Even the dearest that I love the best
   Are strange – nay, rather, stranger than the rest.

I long for scenes where man hath never trod
   A place where woman never smiled or wept
There to abide with my Creator, God,
   And sleep as I in childhood sweetly slept,

> Untroubling and untroubled where I lie
>   The grass below – above, the vaulted sky.

Again the simplicity, the humility of that one word 'Untroubling'; Clare was aware that his life caused difficulties to others, to his wife, his children, even his carers in the asylum. Like Cowper, he knew in his deepest core that he was not made for human companionship and longed for, and found peace only in solitude and amid the loveliness of nature. Here is a poet, troubled beyond what most of us will ever know, who yet peers out of his darkness now and again and grasps with the naturalness of his birth and station the energies of life and creation that he knows are real. His faith continues unquestioning, even in the depths of his wrecking and being wrecked.

> God looks on nature with a glorious eye
> And blesses all creation with the sun
> Its drapery of green and brown, earth, ocean, he
> In morning as Creation just begun
> That saffron East foretells the rising sun
> And who can look upon that majesty
> Of light brightness and splendour nor feel won
> With love of him whose bright all-seeing eye
> Feeds the day's light with Immortality?

Yet this peasant poet, this lost and grieving soul, did not keep his sorrowings out of the poetry. There is a poem where this suffering is given its place and because of the immediacy of his writing and his awareness, the suffering is brought close to us, and we feel it in phrases like 'My bones like hearth-stones burn away', and 'But thou hast held me up awhile and thou hast cast me down'. This poem reads powerfully as it takes into itself all Clare's poetic achievement, all his self-knowledge, all his acute observation, not only of nature and himself, but of the attitude of other people towards him. And the poem ends with the unquestioning acceptance of his fate under the watchful eye of the Creator who has laid all things out:

Lord hear my prayer when trouble glooms
Let sorrow find a way
And when the day of trouble comes
Turn not thy face away
My bones like hearth-stones burn away
My life like vapoury smoke decays

My heart is smitten like the grass
That withered lies and dead
And I so lost to what I was
Forget to eat my bread
My voice is groaning all the day
My bones prick through this skin of clay

The wilderness's pelican
The desert's lonely owl
I am their like, a desert man
In ways as lone and foul
As sparrows on the cottage top
I wait till I with faintness drop

I hear my enemies' reproach
All silently I mourn
They on my private peace encroach
Against me they are sworn
Ashes as bread my trouble shares
And mix my food with weeping cares

Yet not for them is sorrow's toil
I fear no mortal's frown
But thou hast held me up awhile
And thou hast cast me down
My days like shadows waste from view
I mourn like withered grass in dew

But thou Lord shalt endure forever
All generations through
Thou shalt to Zion be the giver
Of joy and mercy too
Her very stones are in their trust
Thy servants reverence her dust

Heathens shall hear and fear thy name
All kings of earth thy glory know
When thou shalt build up Zion's fame
And live in glory there below
He'll not despise their prayers though mute
But still regard the destitute

There is a great deal to be drawn from the lives and works of both Cowper and Clare. Apart from those moments of intense feeling that issue in some of the finest, most direct, intimate and accomplished poems, there is a sense that poetry and religion meet at a level that is surely so deep and genuine that a natural link must be drawn between them. In the greatest suffering both of these men turned to religion but it is not a religion that is merely an escape from suffering: both of them find and show that their moments of greatest human consciousness issue from a religion felt and lived in the marrow of their bones.

The Human Form Divine ...

William Blake (1757-1827)

Blake was born in London and died there. His mind was strongly visual, his writings were illustrated by himself, etched on small copper plates and printed and coloured one by one. He was a difficult man, his judgments penetrating and foolish turn and turn about. He did not try to fit into the world as he knew it, though he supported the American and French Revolutions. Unlike Cowper and Clare, his mind remained acute, his life and living regular, and yet he shared with them a longing that the great masses of the people should share his image of God and of the world. His large and heavy prophetic poems contrast sharply with his gentle lyric voice. His later poems are Christian, loud with biblical overtones, they are visionary warnings and he develops a strongly individual voice. He identified Christ with all spiritual goodness and saw God the Father as a symbol of tyranny. He was very much on the side of individual humans against authority, including the authority of churches and of God the Father. The great prophetic books are difficult, arcane, and require constant reference to explanatory notes. Only a handful of his earlier, simpler lyrics remain readable to the everyday person seeking the marriage of religion and poetry.

The Lamb
> Little Lamb, who made thee?
> Dost thou know who made thee?
Gave thee life, & bid thee feed
By the stream & o'er the mead;
Gave thee clothing of delight,
Softest clothing, wooly, bright;
Gave thee such a tender voice,
Making all the vales rejoice?

Little Lamb, who made thee?
Dost thou know who made thee?

Little Lamb, I'll tell thee,
Little Lamb, I'll tell thee;
He is called by thy name,
For he calls himself a Lamb,
He is meek, & he is mild;
He became a little child.
I, a child, & thou a lamb,
We are called by his name.
Little Lamb, God bless thee!
Little Lamb, God bless thee!

The Divine Image
To Mercy, Pity, Peace, and Love
All pray in their distress;
And to these virtues of delight
Return their thankfulness.

For Mercy, Pity, Peace, and Love
Is God, our father dear,
And Mercy, Pity, Peace, and Love
Is Man, his child and care.

For Mercy has a human heart,
Pity a human face,
And Love, the human form divine,
And Peace, the human dress.

Then every man, of every clime,
That prays in his distress,
Prays to the human form divine,
Love, Mercy, Pity, Peace.

And all must love the human form,
In heathen, turk, or jew;
Where Mercy, Love, & Pity dwell
There God is dwelling too.

The Tyger
Tyger! Tyger! burning bright
In the forests of the night,
What immortal hand or eye
Could frame thy fearful symmetry?

In what distant deeps or skies
Burnt the fire of thine eyes?
On what wings dare he aspire?
What the hand dare seize the fire?

And what shoulder, & what art,
Could twist the sinews of thy heart?
And when thy heart began to beat,
What dread hand? & what dread feet?

What the hammer? what the chain?
In what furnace was thy brain?
What the anvil? what dread grasp
Dare its deadly terrors clasp?

When the stars threw down their spears,
And water'd heaven with their tears,
Did he smile his work to see?
Did he who made the Lamb make thee?

Tyger! Tyger! burning bright
In the forests of the night,
What immortal hand or eye,
Dare frame thy fearful symmetry?

The Garden of Love
I went to the Garden of Love,
And saw what I never had seen:
A Chapel was built in the midst,
Where I used to play on the green.

And the gates of this Chapel were shut,
And 'Thou shalt not' writ over the door;
So I turn'd to the Garden of Love
That so many sweet flowers bore;

And I saw it was filled with graves,
And tomb-stones where flowers should be;
And Priests in black gowns were walking their rounds,
And binding with briars my joys & desires.

A heart breaking for a little love

Christina Rossetti (1830-1894)

Christina Rossetti's father came as a refugee from Naples to England. Christina was born in London and was the younger sister of the more famous Dante Gabriel. All four children of that family became writers. She was educated at home by her mother who had been a governess and was a devout Anglican. She had more Italian friends than English and lived a life of abnegation, the externals of her living being somewhat similar to those of Emily Dickinson though the comparison is, in other respects, not to be too stretched. Christina was a poet of strong emotions, loved the Church of England, her faith a fully accepted one, not questioned. Indeed she appears to have rejected suitors on account of their professed religious faiths or lack of them, so religion itself became more of a comfort to her. She was happy in her friendships and her life centred around her religious practices while her more flamboyant brother won all the fame. Under the pseudonym Ellen Alleyne she contributed some poems to the Pre-Raphaelite journal *The Germ*, founded by her brother William Michael. She tried to help her mother run a school in Somerset but it did not do well. She was a devotee of George Herbert and John Donne. She was never healthy and cardiac troubles came against her later on. Religion, devotion to Jesus, became for her a real consolation.

A Portrait

I

She gave up beauty in her tender youth,
　　Gave up all her hope and joy and pleasant ways,
　　She covered up her eyes lest they should gaze
On vanity, and chose the bitter truth.

Harsh towards herself, towards others full of ruth,
    Servant of servants, little known to praise,
    Long prayers and fasts trenched on her nights and days;
She schooled herself to sights and sounds uncouth
That with the poor and stricken she might make
    A home, until the least of all sufficed
Her wants; her own self learned she to forsake,
Counting all earthly gain but hurt and loss.
So with calm will she chose and bore the cross
    And hated all for love of Jesus Christ.

II
They knelt in silent anguish by her bed,
    And could not weep; but calmly there she lay.
    All pain had left her; and the last sun's ray
Shone through upon her, warming into red
The shady curtains. In her heart she said:
    'Heaven opens; I leave these and go away;
    The Bridegroom calls – shall the Bride seek to stay?'
Then low upon her breast she bowed her head.
O lily flower, O gem of priceless worth,
    O dove with patient voice and patient eyes,
O fruitful vine amid the land of dearth,
    O maid replete with loving purities,
Thou bowedst down thy head with friends on earth
    To raise it with the saints in Paradise.

A Christmas Carol
In the bleak mid-winter
    Frosty wind made moan,
Earth stood hard as iron,
    Water like a stone;
Snow had fallen, snow on snow,
    Snow on snow,
In the bleak mid-winter
    Long ago.

Our God, heaven cannot hold Him
    Nor earth sustain;
Heaven and earth shall flee away
    When he comes to reign:
In the bleak mid-winter
    A stable-place sufficed
The Lord God Almighty
    Jesus Christ.

Enough for Him, whom cherubim
    Worship night and day,
A breastful of milk
    And a mangerful of hay;
Enough for Him, whom angels
    Fall down before,
The ox and camel
    Which adore.

Angels and archangels
    May have gathered there,
Cherubim and seraphim
    Thronged the air;
But only His mother
    In her maiden bliss
Worshipped the Beloved
    With a kiss.

What can I give Him
    Poor as I am?
If I were a shepherd
    I would bring a lamb,
If I were a Wise Man
    I would do my part –
Yet what can I give Him,
    Give my heart.

(It was now time for a return to the more demanding forms
and thoughts of the earlier poets; the work of Rossetti and others

marks the real end of a devotional softness that could not face the real world. Rossetti stands, then, in marked contrast to Emily Dickinson, whose ambience and influences were wholly different yet whose work offers real and demanding responses to the questions of religion and poetry. Blake passed over Rossetti, unheard; and Hopkins was already writing. Poetry and religion poised once again to touch the heights of the earlier writers like Donne and Herbert)

The Mysterious Chaste Bride

Emily Dickinson

Emily Dickinson was born in Amherst, Massachusetts, in 1830 to a family well known for educational and political activity. Her father, an orthodox Calvinist, was a lawyer and treasurer of Amherst College, and also served in Congress. She was educated at Amherst Academy (1834-47) and Mount Holyoke Female Seminary (1847-48). Of her father Emily said, 'You know he never played'. His identification of religious duty with renunciation echoed a lover's martyrdom on Calvary. Emily started writing poems around 1850 and assembled them in packets bound with needle and thread. She guarded her independence jealously and became something of a recluse, spending most of her time in her room. She read a great deal, Keats, Ruskin, Byron and many more. There has been speculation about a possible disappointment in a love affair. Apart from that there is little to report of Emily's life. If she held herself apart from the world going on outside her home, she yet developed an interior life infinitely more deep and powerful than that of so many of her predecessors. She is a strange and very rich phenomenon, emerging from such a dark and delaying world, yet penetrating that world with her own strong and individual grace.

Her emphasis on self-reliance in religion sprang from what she perceived as choice, between a temporal goal or the elusive promise of Christ's heaven. She preferred to take a risk in faith. She never seems to have doubted the existence of God yet often in her work she places herself before him as a child, hoping to hide the desperation of her living and her search. No doubt partly due to a reaction against her father's Calvinism, something grew in her of Byron's sense of rebellion in rejecting a visible church, yet the Jesus she chose to put her faith in was Jesus, the man of grief. She was unhappy with the prevailing Puritan conservative theology. Perhaps one of the great delights in following the development of her religious poetry is that there is no systematic argument behind it; she simply accepts gratefully the moments of joy that come to push the soul along. Yet, because her soul grew in strength and depth, her poetry is by no means static; it keeps pace with her interior growth.

Her work has had a strong influence on modern poetry. The use of dashes, sporadic capitalisations of nouns, her broken metres and unconventional metaphors, all set her out as one of the most innovative poets of nineteenth century American poetry. If she has been seen as a reclusive and eccentric figure, there is no doubt that her intellectual and artistic powers were very strong indeed.

Like Thoreau she focused her thinking on the present, the here and now, coming to tell how the supernatural is disclosed in the everyday. In her peculiar and self-imposed conditions, she came to regard time as one of the most important themes as, in the quiet of her own room, poetry became the centre of her existence. Each of her poems catches on to one of the moments of passing time so that, in ways like Simone Weil, there is no overall design or pattern to her work. Love, too, was a theme, though her beloved existed only in her craving, and she did not allow reality to impinge on that craving. The God she found, and this was a relic of Puritan outlook, was incomprehensible as a Person and remained faceless and menacing for her. Emily Dickinson embodies painful divisions that were evident in the New England mind: the Deity she sought was a kindlier one yet she found her relationship with any Deity intensely problematical. How much this was due to the fact that she closed herself away from any real contact with other human beings, will remain a moot question.

An earlier poem contains still some curiosity about the world of nature beyond her room.

79

Going to Heaven!
I don't know when –
Pray do not ask me how!
Indeed I'm too astonished
To think of answering you!
Going to Heaven!
How dim it sounds!
And yet it will be done
As sure as flocks go home at night
Unto the Shepherd's arm!

Perhaps you're going too!
Who knows?
If you should get there first
Save just a little space for me
Close to the two I lost –
The smallest 'Robe' will fit me
And just a bit of 'Crown' –
For you know we do not mind our dress
When we are going home –

I'm glad I don't believe it
For it would stop my breath –
And I'd like to look a little more
At such a curious Earth!
I'm glad they did believe it
Whom I have never found
Since the mighty Autumn afternoon
I left them in the ground.

This somewhat whimsical piece is a fine mixture of sorrow and playfulness, of simplicity and humility all spiced with a gentle sarcasm. The glory of the poem is that it contradicts itself so gently, in its statement of gladness and its statement of belief – in 'a curious Earth'. This easy tone slips occasionally into the poems but most of the time the work is serious, probing, self-watchful and, from the window of her room gazing out on the people and passing of Amherst, astonishingly wise.

193

I shall know why – when Time is over –
And I have ceased to wonder why –
Christ will explain each separate anguish
In the fair schoolroom of the sky –

He will tell me what 'Peter' promised –
And I – for wonder at his woe –
I shall forget the drop of Anguish
That scalds me now – that scalds me now!

This is no poem of ransom of the present for the sake of a definite future; the tone, again, is too acute for that. Behind what appear to be definite statements in the first half of the poem, and the 'schoolroom' image is richly meaningful here, are hesitancy and uncertainty that urge themselves from the deepest recesses of her being. And what a powerful word is 'scalds', coming as it does after the word 'drop', and the strength and insistence of the phrase leave us in no uncertainty as to the genuineness of that moment's suffering. The Christ featuring in this poem is to be a schoolmaster, instructing ignorant children, children, we feel, who will have many questions and will not accept the answers lightly.

Emily Dickinson grew with her poetry, and it grew along with her, confined though both of them were. It was as if she lived through her poetry, her poems marking off the steps of her life as well as the dates on the calendars. She was real and living only in her poems; words were the source of her strength and the fulfilment of her strength; they were not the results of thought and experience but embodied both as she lived. Her life is the poetry, the poetry is Emily Dickinson. The poems do not fill with objects and events, except those of her own inner life; and some of those events were her responses to the notion of God and another life better than this one. They outline, not the milestones of her journey, but the whole almost invisible curve of that journey, but from where to where? Inside we are all the same, in spite of lives filled with travel, incident, and excitement. Emily Dickinson speaks for us all.

There is, too, that gentle cynicism about the whole heaven matter, expressed in a rather coy humour here and there in the poems:

I think just how my shape will rise –
When I shall be *'forgiven'* –
Till Hair – and Eyes – and timid Head –
Are *out of sight* – in Heaven –

where her dashes and inverted commas and italics and capital letters all lend themselves to that mood and tone of quiet mockery of the whole idea. When, she says, she is finally ready for that great journey to the next life, by horse and carriage, she will ask:

Put me in on the firmest side –
So I shall never fall –
For we must ride to the Judgment –
And it's partly, down Hill –

Her difficult and demanding father, together with the difficult and demanding Puritan outlook on life, kept her sense of religion one of gloom and sadness. This she wished to reject, but the ambivalence and doubt remained with her and peppered the poems in this still early stage of her poetry and life.

413

I never felt at Home – Below –
And in the Handsome Skies
I shall not feel at Home – I know –
I don't like Paradise –

Because it's Sunday – all the time –
And Recess – never comes –
And Eden'll be so lonesome
Bright Wednesday Afternoons –

If God could make a visit –
Or ever took a Nap –
So not to see us – but they say
Himself – a Telescope –

Perennial beholds us –
Myself would run away
From Him – and Holy Ghost – and All –
But there's the 'Judgment day'!

At this stage she is still prepared to think of religion as schooling and God as a perpetually watching Head teacher; the only escape from the dimness of Sunday rigidity is to run away, to mitch from it all. But there is sin, there is judgment, there is hell! Or is there? Quickly, the sadness and emptiness of her life, apart from her own room and her poetry, placed a weight of sorrow on her spirit, a sense of the hard journey that life is. One of her most powerful poems takes up again that theme of horse and carriage to take the soul away; it adds in the notion of school and holiday, the loveliness of the world, however small the garden and acreage she knew and allowed herself to know, with that heavy awareness that mortality is not a childhood game, but a reality.

712

Because I could not stop for Death –
He kindly stopped for me –
The Carriage held but just Ourselves –
And Immortality.

We slowly drove – He knew no haste
And I had put away
My labour and my leisure too,
For His Civility –

We passed the School, where Children strove
At Recess – in the Ring –
We passed the Fields of Gazing Grain –
We passed the Setting Sun –

Or rather – He passed Us –
The Dews drew quivering and chill –
For only Gossamer, my Gown –
My Tippet – only Tulle –

We paused before a House that seemed
A Swelling of the Ground –
The Roof was scarcely visible –
The Cornice – in the Ground –

Since then – 'tis Centuries – and yet
Feels shorter than the Day
I first surmised the Horses' Heads
Were toward Eternity –

There is an unmissable echo of George Herbert's poem *Love* in another of Emily's poems, a rather whimsical echo, where the hesitation and the doubt are more palpable than the final sense of acceptance of God's unquestioning generosity that is found in Herbert.

964

'Unto Me?' I do not know you –
Where may be your House?

'I am Jesus – Late of Judea –
New – of Paradise' –

Wagons – have you – to convey me?
This is far from Thence –

'Arms of Mine – sufficient Phaeton –
Trust Omnipotence' –

I am spotted – 'I am Pardon' –
I am small – 'The Least
Is esteemed in Heaven the Chiefest –
Occupy my House' –

This is, as is Herbert's poem, a reasoning with one's self, and a willing that the answer may be love, and generosity beyond what our human nature may expect. And so her life and poetry pass, and the temptation is to see Emily Dickinson all the time sad and alone and removed from the world, looking into the mirror of her own spirit and stitching away at her poetry. And so, no doubt, a great deal of her life was spent. But there are moments of sparkle and light, as there are in all our lives, in spite of the 'I am spotted' and 'I am small' of the poem just quoted. And in the development of her sense of God, there are moments of light, too, but they are rare and are always darkened by her unsureness. For her, life is no miracle; the sunlight may filter in through the chintz curtains on the windows of her room; every now and then she may wander to the edges of Amherst, or through the nearby orchard, or into the meadows where the world offers its own miracles of growth, colour and change. But is it not the greatest sadness that we do not make the leap of faith, that we do not take the chance and offer our lives to the miracle: the miracle of the possibility of heaven, to the possibility of a full life fully lived? It appears to be the fact that the way such a faith in life and eternity is presented to us, will determine the way we react to that telling. If it is conveyed with a love that one is sensually aware of, if it is presented with a positive and joyful earnestness, rather than a dour and demanding portentousness, then the possibilities of answering positively are more sure; in things of the spirit 'I am small': and the Christ told us that it is the children, those of unquestioning and selfless acceptance, that will inherit the kingdom.

1258
Who were 'the Father and the Son'
We pondered when a child,
And what had they to do with us
And when portentous told

With inference appalling
By Childhood fortified
We thought, at least they are no worse
Than they have been described.

Who are 'the Father and the Son'
Did we demand Today
'The Father and the Son' himself
Would doubtless specify –

But had they the felicity
When we desired to know,
We better Friends had been, perhaps,
Than time ensue to be –

We start – to learn that we believe
But once – entirely –
Belief, it does not fit so well
When altered frequently –

We blush, that Heaven if we achieve –
Event ineffable –
We shall have shunned until ashamed
To own the Miracle –

This poem has a slowness and sad awareness to it that has
thrown out all the little bits of humour and irony the earlier
work had allowed in to her poems of faith and seeking. The
doubt is still there, but the sense that life would have been much
more fruitful if the faith had been well presented to her at the beginning, is a deeply tragic sense of loss and wastefulness. Her
growing awareness of the weakness of her own faith and her
wish to have a much stronger belief, deepen the later poems and
slows them to a kind of dirge, where the lines plod heavily, even
though they remain short, the rhymes are much less full, thus
creating a sense of unease in the reading:

1433
How brittle are the Piers
On which our Faith doth tread –
No Bridge below doth totter so –
Yet none hath such a Crowd.

It is as old as God –
Indeed – 'twas built by him –
He sent his Son to test the Plank,
And he pronounced it firm.

That word 'firm' is rich with irony, I believe; and the Plank
that God sent his Son to 'test' surely reminds the reader of the
wood of the cross; faith then depends on such suffering, it must
take that same 'test' and if the firmness is there, then perhaps we
shall not 'totter' so much on the bridge we have to cross.

As her quiet life progressed this sense of condemnation and
evil associated with belief in God, remained strong in Emily's
mind as if she continued in an effort of belief, but found the negativities she was introduced to as a child always daunting.

1545
The Bible is an antique Volume –
Written by faded Men
At the suggestion of Holy Spectres –
Subjects – Bethlehem –
Eden – the ancient Homestead –
Satan – the Brigadier –
Judas – the Great Defaulter –
David – the Troubadour –
Sin – a distinguished Precipice
Others must resist –
Boys that 'believe' are very lonesome –
Other Boys are 'lost' –
Had but the Tale a warbling Teller –
All the Boys would come –
Orpheus' Sermon captivated –
It did not condemn –

Heaven remains in her mind closely associated with that
place to which she should be brought by horse and carriage, a
homestead, yet it was in that homestead that faith was first
linked to condemnation for her. Now it is clear that faith for
Emily Dickinson would have been easier if it had been presented

in a more human and humane fashion, if it had been offered in terms of epic or myth, as the Orpheus story is presented. It will always be impossible to know if she might have developed her faith if she had gone out 'into the world' and lived a more traditional life style, had a job, had a family, mixed with people whose faith was stronger. The opposite, indeed, held sway as a late poem testifies.

> 1551
> Those – dying then,
> Knew where they went –
> They went to God's Right Hand –
> That Hand is amputated now
> And God cannot be found –
>
> The abdication of Belief
> Makes the Behaviour small –
> Better an ignis fatuus
> Than no illume at all –

What a sad conclusion she has come to! And there is another piece, also late in her life and writing, where she sees life as a prison, even though it may be a magical one; life itself has not allowed her the happiness she knows would have been possible; and if, in her sidelined living, there have been faults, she pleads for forgiveness, but in a vague, uncertain way. And finally, what happiness she may have known has been undershot all through her living by the early negativities she found thrust upon her. It is to our gladness that Emily Dickinson spent her life in the small room of her poetry, a room that has expanded through the honesty of the self-examination she conducted through her poems into a universe we all might better understand.

> 1601
> Of God we may ask one favour,
> That we may be forgiven –
> For what, he is presumed to know –
> The Crime, from us, is hidden –

Immured the whole of Life
Within a magic Prison
We reprimand the Happiness
That too competes with Heaven.

The depth and integrity of her self-probing has resulted in a poetry that we may all inhabit, a special room, immaculately kept, where her soul struggled with innumerable doubts and hopes and fears, and with an early sense of sin and guilt imposed on her from without. Those of us who have spent our lives in the wild and rushing world, who still find guilt and a need for forgiveness holding our minds in some thrall, need but follow and understand that long and wonderfully productive journey Emily Dickinson made within her poetry.

The Expectation of the Creature
Gerard Manley Hopkins

Here is a famous passage, often taken with a truck-load of salt, from St Paul, in Romans, 8:18; 'For I reckon that the sufferings of the present time are not worthy to be compared with the glory which shall be revealed in us. For the earnest expectation of the creature waits for the manifestation of the sons of God. For the creature was made subject to vanity, not willingly, but by reason of him who has subjected the same in hope, because the creature itself also shall be delivered from the bondage of corruption into the glorious liberty of the children of God. For we know that the whole creation groans and labours in pain together until now. And not only they, but ourselves also, who have the firstfruits of the Spirit, even we ourselves groan within ourselves, waiting for the adoption, namely, the redemption of our body.' Now, I have no direct proof that Hopkins relished this passage but from his notebooks, his sermons and devotional writings, and of course from his poems, there is no doubt that his love of beauty, of nature, of the physical things and patterns of the world, took on more than a sacramental force. The world outside the self in its redemptive quality and its loveliness praises God; hence it is all a question of incarnation: being in the Flesh. In that strange and wonderful poem, *That Nature is a Heraclitean Fire and of the comfort of the Resurrection* this is manifest: 'Million-fuelèd, nature's bonfire burns on.' And man is the glory of this creation. Hopkins goes on to consider the sad fact of the death of the human: 'nor mark / Is any of him at all so stark / But vastness blurs and time beats level.' This was written soon after the sufferings outlined in the 'terrible sonnets' and at this point in the poem, his technique flexes all its muscles, then falls to simplicity until the will takes over in 'Enough! the Resurrection'. The fact of his faith in the Christ leads him to the conclusion that man will be

'Immortal diamond'. I believe that deep within him he thought the same, in some form, of nature itself, as Paul outlined in the above passage. After all it is man who has sullied the face and fact of nature's beauty:

Generations have trod, have trod, have trod;
    And all is seared with trade; bleared, smeared with toil;
    And wears man's smudge and shares man's smell: the soil
Is bare now, nor can foot feel, being shod.

And for all this, nature is never spent;
    There lives the dearest freshness deep down things ...

And how does this occur?

    Because the Holy Ghost over the bent
    World broods with warm breast and with ah! bright wings.
(God's Grandeur)

So many of Hopkins's poems, particularly after the great resurgence of his work when *The Wreck of the Deutschland* had liberated his powers, are simple revelling in the glory and worth of nature, each poem leading on from this to a glorying of God, the creator. Hopkins sees God as master, nature as fresh and fruitful, and man in need of redemption. The implication, inevitably, is that nature is not in need of this form of redemption but partakes already of that dear freshness and renewal that leads the human being who is aware of it, directly to God. The world itself, the physical universe, is shot through with sanctity; it is the bones of God, the body of Christ, it is the atmosphere we breathe in and breathe out.

There are two lesser-loved poems by Gerard Manley Hopkins, *The Blessed Virgin compared to the Air we Breathe*, and *Tom's Garland*, both of which I believe will offer an entry into an unexplored field of this powerful poet's work.

The Blessed Virgin compared to the Air we Breathe
Wild air, world-mothering air,
Nestling me everywhere,
That each eyelash or hair
Girdles; goes home betwixt
The Fleeciest, frailest-flixed
Snowflake; that's fairly mixed
With, riddles, and is rife
In every least thing's life;
This needful, never spent,
And nursing element;
My more than meat and drink,
My meal at every wink;
This air, which, by life's law,
My lung must draw and draw
Now but to breathe its praise,
Minds me in many ways
Of her who not only
Gave God's infinity
Dwindled to infancy
Welcome in womb and breast,
Birth, milk, and all the rest
But mothers each new grace
That does now reach our race –
Mary Immaculate,
Merely a woman, yet
Whose presence, power is
Great as no goddess's
Was deemèd, dreamèd; who
This one work has to do –
Let all God's glory through,
God's glory which would go
Through her and from her flow
Off, and no way but so.
      I say that we are wound
With mercy round and round

As if with air: the same
Is Mary, more by name.
She, wild web, wondrous robe,
Mantles the guilty globe,
Since God has let dispense
His prayers his providence:
Nay, more than almoner,
The sweet alms' self is her
And men are meant to share
Her life as life does air.

    If I have understood,
She holds high motherhood
Towards all our ghostly good
And plays in grace her part
About man's beating heart,
Laying, like air's fine flood,
The deathdance in his blood;
Yet no part but what will
Be Christ our Saviour still.
Of her flesh he took flesh:
He does take fresh and fresh,
Though much the mystery how,
Not flesh but spirit now
And makes, O marvellous!
New Nazareths in us,
Where she shall yet conceive
Him, morning, noon, and eve;
New Bethlems, and he born
There, evening, noon, and morn –
Bethlem or Nazareth,
Men here may draw like breath
More Christ and baffle death;
Who, born so, comes to be
New self and nobler me
In each one and each one
More makes, when all is done,

Both God's and Mary's Son.
        Again, look overhead
How air is azurèd;
O how! Nay do but stand
Where you can lift your hand
Skywards: rich, rich it laps
Round the four fingergaps.
Yet such a sapphire-shot,
Charged, steepèd sky will not
Stain light. Yea, mark you this:
It does no prejudice.
The glass-blue days are those
When every colour glows,
Each shape and shadow shows.
Blue be it: this blue heaven
The seven or seven times seven
Hued sunbeam will transmit
Perfect, not alter it.
Or if there does some soft,
On things aloof, aloft,
Bloom breathe, that one breath more
Earth is the fairer for.
Whereas did air not make
This bath of blue and slake,
A blear and blinding ball
With blackness bound, and all
The thick stars round him roll
Flashing like flocks of coal,
Quartz-fret, or sparks of salt,
In grimy vasty vault.
        Be thou then, O thou dear
Mother, my atmosphere;
My happier world, wherein
To wend and meet no sin;
Above me, round me lie
Fronting my froward eye

With sweet and scarless sky;
Stir in my ears, speak there
Of God's love, O live air,
Of patience, penance, prayer:
World-mothering air, air wild,
Wound with thee, in thee isled,
Fold home, fast fold thy child.

Not the greatest poem he wrote, without doubt, tending too much towards the devotional, dutiful work than to 'the roll, the rise, the carol, the creation'. But there are some things in it worth noting. Firstly, this tendency to write betimes out of a sense of duty or devotion I believe has slightly damaged one of his greatest poems, and to this I shall return. And secondly, it is worth taking cognisance of the early part of the poem where the air, 'world-mothering air', is given many lines of devotion in itself. To compare Mary to the air, he first must show the value of air in itself and, of course, for Hopkins the things of this world were marvellous in themselves. Further on in the poem he returns to this, with an easier mastery than in the rest of the poem: 'Again, look overhead …' There is at once a more fluid and happy tone in this passage, and some of the special Hopkins awareness that leads to an excitement of language and imagery: 'Rich it laps / Round the four fingergaps. / Yet such a sapphire-shot, / Charged, steepèd sky will not / Stain light.' What I am implying is that the physical universe, the beauty of the world, so touched and lifted Hopkins's spirit that it was almost a climb-down for him to draw the morals from it that his priesthood directed him to draw.

Take, here, an earlier poem, and read it without its 'subtitle'. This early poem was first called *Rest*, a bland but meaningful title; that was changed to *Fair Havens, or The Convent*, the first part excellent, the second part limiting; it eventually became *Heaven-Haven*, a delightful name in itself, but already tending to limit the poem's universal appeal. If the poem is taken simply as *Fair Havens* it reaches to a far greater width of meaning:

I have desired to go
    Where springs not fail,
To fields where flies no sharp and sided hail
    And a few lilies blow.

And I have asked to be
    Where no storms come,
Where the green swell is in the havens dumb,
    And out of the swing of the sea.

A fine lyric in its own right, full of an exact awareness of
nature's movements, echoed in a choice of words and rhythms
that leave the reader wholly satisfied. But now, that subtitle, 'A
nun takes the veil'! Oh dear, how it limits the poem, how it
draws it away from universal meaning to a sadly diminished
power; and we have always been led to believe that the taking of
religious vows was not to be an escape from the world, but a
more whole and generous giving of the self to God's presence in
that world. Already a sense of guilt and duty tends to thwart the
wider movement of Hopkins's poetry, shifting it from a natural
love of the world around him, to a willed pushing of the poem
towards religious morals.

Another poem I wish to focus attention on is *Tom's Garland*: a
poem which carries a legitimate subtitle, 'upon the Unemployed':

Tom – garlanded with squat and surly steel
Tom; then Tom's fallowbootfellow piles pick
By him and rips out rockfire homeforth – sturdy Dick;
Tom Heart-at-ease, Tom Navvy: he is all for his meal
Sure, 's bed now. Low be it: lustily he his low lot (feel
That ne'er need hunger, Tom; Tom seldom sick,
Seldomer heartsore; that treads through, prickproof, thick
Thousands of thorns, thoughts) swings through.
        Commonweal
Little I reck ho! lacklevel in, if all had bread:
What! Country is honour enough in all us – lordly head,
With heaven's lights high hung round, or, mother-ground
That mammocks, mighty foot. But no way sped,

Nor mind nor mainstrength; gold go garlanded
With, perilous, O no; nor yet plod safe shod sound;
                    Undenizened, beyond bound
Of earth's glory, earth's ease, all; no one, nowhere,
In wide the world's weal; rare gold, bold steel, bare
                    In both; care, but share care –
This, by Despair, bred Hangdog dull; by Rage,
Manwolf, worse; and their packs infest the age.

Hopkins was, at this stage, in fairly good spirits again after
the depression and illness that brought him to write the 'terrible
sonnets', yet he still complained that he lacked inspiration
enough to go further than the sonnet form. This is one of those
'sonnets' that yet manage to break the mould and push it to its
limits, and beyond. The friends to whom he sent it could not figure it out at all and he sent the following 'crib' to Bridges; what I
am interested in highlighting here is the idea of 'commonwealth' that Hopkins outlines, and relates to the St Paul idea of
humanity as being one body, of which the head is Christ, and
how all this points back to the Pauline notion I mentioned at the
start of this essay, of the whole world being one:

It means then that, as St Paul and Plato and Hobbes and
everybody says, the commonwealth or well ordered human
society is like one man; a body with many members and each
its function; some higher, some lower, but all honourable,
from the honour which belongs to the whole. The head is the
sovereign, who has no superior but God and from heaven re-
ceives his or her authority: we must then imagine this head
as bare (see St Paul much on this) and covered, so to say, only
with the sun and stars, of which the crown is a symbol, which
is an ornament but not a covering; it has an enormous hat or
skull cap, the vault of heaven. The foot is the daylabourer,
and this is armed with hobnail boots, because it has to wear
and to be worn by the ground; which again is symbolical; for
it is navvies or daylabourers who, on the great scale or in
gangs and millions, mainly trench, tunnel, blast, and in other
ways disfigure, 'mammock' the earth and, on a small scale,

singly, and superficially stamp it with the footprints. And the 'garlands' of nails they wear are therefore the visible badge of the place they fill, the lowest in the commonwealth. But this place still shares the common honour, and if it wants one advantage, glory or public fame, makes up for it by another, ease of mind, absence of care; and these things are symbolised by the gold and the iron garlands. (O, once explained, how clear it all is!) Therefore the scene of the poem is laid at evening, when they are giving over work and one after another pile their picks, with which they earn their living, and swing off home, knocking sparks out of mother earth not now by labour and of choice but by the mere footing, being strongshod and making no hardship of hardness, taking all easy. And so to supper and bed. Here comes a violent but effective hyperbaton or suspension, in which the action of the mind mimics that of the labourer – surveys his lot, low but free from care; then by a sudden strong act throws it over the shoulder or tosses it away as light matter. The witnessing of which lightheartedness makes me indignant with the fools of Radical Levellers. But presently I remember that this is all very well for those who are in, however low in, the Commonwealth and share in any way the Common weal; but that the curse of our times is that many do not share it, that they are outcasts from it and have neither security nor splendour; that they share care with the high and obscurity with the low, but wealth or comfort with neither. And this state of things, I say, is the origin of Loafers, Tramps, Cornerboys, Roughs, Socialists and other pests of society. And I think that it is a very pregnant sonnet and in point of execution very highly wrought. Too much so, I am afraid.'

The 'crib' speaks for itself and leaves a feeling of satisfaction that brings the poem very much to light, and very much into the heart of Hopkins's poetry. What interests me here is Hopkins's sense of 'Commonwealth'; this is more than a political entity, rather it is closer to St Paul's sense of the world being 'one body' and that the curse of our times is that not everybody is willing to share in this general working for the benefit of all. And in this, because of Hopkins's sense of, and love of, nature in general, I believe that Hopkins saw all of creation as one, as the work of God's creating, and that all points to God and all works towards God's approbation and ultimate reward.

So we go back to *The Wreck of the Deutschland* where God's physical and spiritual nearness is manifest, not only in the individual soul's labouring towards God, but in the presence of nature itself:

> Thou hast bound bones and veins in me, fastened me flesh,
> And after it almost unmade, what with dread,
>   Thy doing: and dost thou touch me afresh?
> Over again I feel thy finger and find thee.

And then he salutes nature as leading him towards a closer communion with God:

>   I kiss my hand
>   To the stars, lovely-asunder
> Starlight, wafting him out of it; and
>   Glow, glory in thunder;
> Kiss my hand to the dappled-with-damson west:
> Since, tho' he is under the world's splendour and wonder,
>   His mystery must be instressed, stressed;
> For I greet him the days I meet him, and bless when I understand.

Even without being aware, as we all are unaware most of the time, of God's presence being served and worshipped in the things of nature, Hopkins gloried in nature for its own sake. Having already written of and assumed the presence of God behind the glory of things, he came to that most 'pagan', meaning directly nature-informed, poem, *The Windhover*. Read it first without that dedication, which was added as a guilty afterthought: Hopkins was fiercely and sadly scrupulous when it came to his faith and his priesthood and felt that nothing he wrote or said should appear removed from God's service:

The Windhover

I caught this morning morning's minion, king-
   dom of daylight's dauphin, dapple-dawn-drawn Falcon
         in his riding
Of the rolling level underneath him steady air, and striding
High there, how he rung upon the rein of a wimpling wing
In his ecstasy! then off, off forth on swing,
   As a skate's heel sweeps smooth on a bow-bend: the hurl and
         gliding
Rebuffed the big wind. My heart in hiding
Stirred for a bird – the achieve of, the mastery of the thing!

Brute beauty and valour and act, oh, air, pride, plume, here
   Buckle! AND the fire that breaks from thee then, a billion
Times told lovelier, more dangerous, O my chevalier!

No wonder of it: sheer plod makes plough down sillion
Shine, and blue-bleak embers, ah my dear,
   Fall, gall themselves, and gash gold-vermilion.

Hopkins later wrote, 'That is the best thing I ever wrote.' This is simple, exquisite and complete revelling in the perfection of act and being that nature can display in the utter mastery of its environment by this bird, the kestrel. There is clearly evident Hopkins's own longing to achieve such a mastery of the world in which he lived. I do not want to get into all the controversy about the meaning and focus of the imagery of 'dauphin' etc., but simply to concentrate on Hopkins's delight in this poem. In front of such mastery he is wholly aware of his own hesitations and imperfections, 'my heart in hiding', envied the mastery of the bird. There is no other interpretation of the 'thee' of this poem than that he is addressing his own heart. In many other poems Hopkins addressed himself:

'Ah, touched in your bower of bone, / Are you! turned for an exquisite smart, / Have you! make words break from me here all alone, / Do you! – mother of being in me, heart ...' 'What hours, O what black hours we have spent / This night! what sighs you, heart, saw; ways you went! ...' 'My own heart let me more have pity on ...'

In *The Windhover* he is urging his heart to become lovelier and more dangerous a chevalier than even the bird can become and this is done and achieved only through suffering, effort, and an ever greater effort. The fact that he later added the dedication *To Christ our Lord* has merely salved his own conscience and thrown critics and commentators into a frenzy of searching and explanation beyond the poem's core.

It is certain that Christ was the centre of Hopkins's world; I do not even begin to deny that. But it is the unity of creation and what it may achieve when perfectly in action and in harmony with itself, and when men are also in harmony with nature, that this poem celebrates. The basis for this 'oneness' of the whole world is, in Hopkins's view, the Real Presence in the Eucharist. In a letter to his old schoolfriend, E. H. Coleridge, on 1 June 1864, Hopkins said that the main object of Christian belief was the doctrine of the Real Presence: that is belief in the actual presence of Christ's body and blood in the Eucharist. It was this that brought him to Catholicism. In the summer of 1872 Hopkins began to read Duns Scotus, the thirteenth century Franciscan philosopher who had perhaps the greatest single impact on his mature thought, and developed and clarified Hopkins's sense of individuation, and that this individuation still was held in oneness. Over all this world the Holy Ghost 'broods with warm breast and with ah! bright wings'. Duns Scotus held a somewhat heretical belief that the incarnation would have happened even without Adam's fall; this gives a glory to the whole material world, allowing Hopkins a sort of Pagan faith as in *Pied Beauty, God's Grandeur, Starlight Night, Hurrahing in Harvest*, as well as and most of all in *The Windhover*.

In the *Spiritual Writings* Hopkins has: 'I find myself both as man and as myself something most determined and distinctive, at pitch, more distinctive and higher pitched than anything else I see; I find myself with pleasures and pains, my powers and my experiences, my deserts and guilt, my shame and sense of beauty, my dangers, hopes, fears, and all my fate, more important to myself than anything I see. And when I ask where does all this throng and stack of being, so rich, so distinctive, so important, come from / nothing I see can answer me ... For human nature, being more highly pitched, selved, and distinctive than anything in the world, can have been developed, evolved, condensed, from the vastness of the world not anyhow or by the working of common powers but only by one of finer or higher pitch and determination than itself and certainly than any that elsewhere we see, for this power had to force forward the starting or stubborn elements to the one pitch required.'

                Across my foundering deck shone
A beacon, an eternal beam. Flesh fade, and mortal trash
Fall to the residuary worm; world's wildfire, leave but ash:
                In a flash, at a trumpet crash,
I am all at once what Christ is, since he was what I am, and
This Jack, joke, poor potsherd, patch, matchwood, immortal
     diamond,
                Is immortal diamond.

The Hoard of the Imagination

*(A talk presented at the Merriman Summer School, Lisdoonvarna,
2005, with thanks to Bob Collins)*

As a nation, poetry has been important for us; even the individual poet can be made to feel, on occasion, a little important. And
yet a new collection of poetry is almost wholly disregarded. In a
time of unparalleled prosperity in Ireland, I find myself de-
pressed by the direction and thrust of what this loved country is
doing, loved because I have lived and grown up in it and taken
its pith and sap into my own pith and sap, yet those very qualities with which I have identified my love are being so rapidly
and thoughtlessly thrown over. The word 'decadent' occurs; not
a word often applied to this country that has only recently
emerged from centuries of occupation. Decadence is a falling
away, from what? From an adherence to values of love and
faithfulness, and to poetry. We are still an adolescent country,
now for the first time in our history I believe we find ourselves
deprived of a real purpose or meaning in life, we are given over
to the owning of properties. I know there is no once-and-for-all
defining and delimiting kerygma or message: faith in something
is a decision to be taken over and over again, to be renewed, re-
articulated, re-visited. There is perpetually needed a new and
renewing imaginative examination of where we are, as individ-
uals, as a country. The events of our lives need to be epiphanied.

Affirmation of the moment, the place, the here, the now – this
is poetry – not the fact of its commercial or non-commercial
value or use. A poem is an epiphany, interrupting the flow. A
good new collection of poetry slips like the Magi into the ongoing thrust of the world, interrupting, often with its strangeness,
the destructive aims of a Herod. The life of poetry will depend
on whether or not we wish to have that flow interrupted.
Imagine for a moment, that old stable or cave, the birth of a baby

boy, the rumours surrounding that birth, the search for a child perceived as so threatening to the *status quo* of the Roman presence in Palestine. Imagine the arrival of three strange beings 'come from afar', seeking a new King whose star they have seen in the east. Herod's confusion; his unsubtle request that they show him where this child is that he, too, might come and adore. And the way the three slipped away from him back into their own utterly altered lives. The event, the epiphany, is poetry in its fluid existence; the imagining of the event is poetry, too. And if this imagining is rejected, so too is the poetry, and the *status quo* returns with a grateful gush.

Let me put a poem before you, one of my own:

Nightwatch
In our suburban villages, our dormitory towns
we lie secure. But at the city's core
up and down the crack-tiled steps of the men's
shelter, they pass who could be minister

or president or priest – but are not;
in dust-striped suits and mismatched waistcoats
who could be civil servants – but are not;
greased and creased and ill at ease they ghost,

side-staggering, our streets, who might
be Plato, Luther, Hopkins but for some tiny thing
that slipped and shifted them a little to the side.
Their dream is a coin found under slanting

light, oblivion enough to damp down care
a while. But wish us all good health and reason
who wake sometimes, knowing we too have been
visited by importunate ghosts and have forgotten;

tell us what we dreamed, interpret for us the dream.

Notice how a great deal of the history told in the Bible occurs because of dreams listened to and obeyed. In first century Palestine it was a crime to become pregnant before marriage, a crime punishable by stoning to death. There was a young man named Joseph and he was betrothed to a young woman, Mary; imagine his suffering when he found that the woman he loved was already with child. The young man, according to the law, had to denounce her; these are the words in Deuteronomy: 'They shall bring the young woman out to the entrance of her father's house and the men of her town shall stone her to death because she committed a disgraceful act ... So you shall purge the evil from your midst.' How was he to behave? Then came that dream and an angel spoke to him in his dream and Joseph was a changed and loyal person from then on. And there was that other dream, another angel coming to tell him to get Mary and the child out of there and flee to Egypt. A dream, or a vision to which he was once more obedient. And they stayed in exile until a third dream brought them back. What is all this following of dreams? Imagine, imagine how the world would have been other without these interventions!

There was Jacob who set out to find his lover and on the way had to spend a night sleeping in the open desert; he took a stone for pillow and had a most wonderful dream, angels of God ascending and descending on a ladder fixed between heaven and earth. Here, too, is the dream forewarning, urging the dreamer to take the path of foolishness. And long before that again there was another Joseph, he of the amazing coloured dream-coat, whose dreams of dominance got him into trouble with his brothers and he, too, found himself, because of dreams, exiled to Egypt. Eventually he came to interpret the dreams of the Pharaoh and thus saved the land in which he was an exile from famine years, becoming, in the process, the most powerful man in Egypt, next to the Pharaoh. And what do we remember most about that man? His dreams, and the power of interpretation.

More than Joseph even, with his Pharaoh, there was Daniel. That proud king, Nebuchodonosor, had such a vivid dream that when he woke he could remember nothing of it save that it was horrific. Nobody could tell him what he had dreamt (how could they?) so he had his wisest men put to death. Until our wee Daniel came along, told him what he had dreamed and inter-

preted the dream for him, thus ensuring that Nebuchodonosor
held his throne; Daniel. This imaginative story gave an urgency
to the poem I have quoted already,

> wish us all good health and reason
> who wake sometimes, knowing we too have been
> visited by importunate ghosts and have forgotten;

> tell us what we dreamed, interpret for us the dream.

There is a part of us, the dreaming part, the imagining part,
where we may well have powers to interpret things we do not
understand and by acting on those barely understood things, to
change the course of history, our personal history and the
greater one. These are imaginative responses; they are epiphanies; they are entrances into what is called 'real life' by another
level; they are the entrances of the wisdom and wonder of the
magi into the bleak realities of the stable. And both our religious
living and our everyday economies have been suffering because
of the lack of such imaginative entries.

We are celebrating the great work of Brian Merriman. The response of so many poets to the penal laws and the crime of men-
tioning the name of Ireland was the Aisling, the dream or vision
poem that kept the hope alive; Merriman's work takes off from
poetry as dream, becomes its own epiphany, pushing its way
with aggrieved ceremony and insistent otherness into a world of
clerical dominance and patristic overweening, and does so with
a cock-of-the-snook humour and the certainties of the poem's
form. Subversive, bold and disarming. Perhaps Plato, longing
for a well-ordered community, was right when he insisted that
he would banish all poets from any rightly ordered community.
Poetry is an instrument of disorder, but of a disorder that urges
towards a finer, more humanity-serving, order.

The Book of Revelation is one that has remained compulsive
in the power of its imagery and the august yet sideways questioning of the morality of all humanity. And, of course, the
whole thing is a dream. Chapter 7 begins: 'After this, I beheld
four angels standing at the four corners of the earth, holding fast

the four winds of the earth.' These words set up a vital image from which the writer can proceed to utter threats and warnings to a world gone morally askew. John Donne takes up this dream and makes it his own:

At the round earth's imagin'd corners, blow
Your trumpets, Angels, and arise, arise
From death, you numberless infinities
Of souls, and to your scattered bodies go,
All whom the flood did, and fire shall o'erthrow,
All whom war, dearth, age, agues, tyrannies,
Despair, law, chance, hath slain, and you whose eyes
Shall behold God, and never taste death's woe.
But let them sleep, Lord, and me mourn a space,
For, if above all these my sins abound,
'Tis late to ask abundance of thy grace,
When we are there; here on this lowly ground,
Teach me how to repent; for that's as good
As if thou'hadst seal'd my pardon, with thy blood.

He begins by remarking that the vision is already an imagined one, the 'round earth's imagined corners', and so appropriates the book of Revelation to his concerns. He then introduces two great 'if's. 'If above all these my sins abound', offers to the Lord the sinner's self-awareness and humility, but without insisting on it, and thus pleading for Divine aid; there is no question here that the poet regards himself indeed as a greater sinner than all others, because that 'if' stands strong and sure at the gateway to the suggestion. He goes on to plead for time, because, the suggestion remains, he has not yet repented, nor does he know how; 'Teach me how to repent', he says, and all of this thrusts yet towards the future. The poem ends on the second 'if', learning to repent would be just as good as if the Christ had sealed his pardon with Christ's blood. The point is, of course, that this blood has already been spilled, the pardon has been sealed, the author is aware of it but allows the whole thing to hang loose, between that great and final 'as if' and the beginning of the poem, 'the round earth's imagined corners'.

Donne's irony and humour create his own unique and subtly powerful way of entering our imagination and subverting our perceptions and self-gratulations. His 'Holy Sonnets' hang wonderfully between his secular longings for success and sexual conquests, and the obligations to his immortal soul of which he is aware. This is a poetry exemplary of the lasting power of the imagination to get under the integuments of our living, to disrupt us in our easy ongoing sense of where we are in relation to this world, its ending, and the demands of the next, imagined, world.

A person's life, as we know, is not composed of a series of spectacular events, though such are the events we tend to remember. But the uneventful moments, turning the angle of a street, lifting a cup to the lips, when suddenly a memory will rise unbidden, the surfacing of a similar moment of no seeming importance when it occurred, but that now takes the lord mayor's place in the city hall of memory: it is of moments like these that a life is composed, moments which, if carefully examined, may reveal the deepest, certainly the most lasting, compounding details of a life. These are 'epiphanies', moments that take their place in the making of a complete human being. There is a poem by Thomas Kinsella that makes a sacrarium of such a moment. It is called *Hen Woman*. The poem begins with a stanza that seems to set up an event of some importance:

The noon heat in the yard
smelled of stillness and coming thunder.
A hen scratched and picked at the shore.
It stopped, its body crouched and puffed out.
The brooding silence seemed to say 'Hush ...'

That word 'brooding' contains both the waiting thunder, and the possibility of the appearance of an egg. The door opens and the observer hears a clock; the poem remarks, in parenthesis, *(I had felt all this before ...)* An old lady emerges, angry that the hen is about to lay in a disordered fashion, and she grabs for the hen just as the white egg appears. This is the moment when time seems to stop for the observer, when every tiny detail of the moment is remembered:

There was a tiny movement at my feet,
tiny and mechanical; I looked down.
A beetle like a bronze leaf
was inching across the cement,
clasping with small tarsi
a ball of dung bigger than its body.
The serrated brow pressed the ground humbly,
lifted in a short stare, bowed again;
the dung-ball advanced minutely,
losing a few fragments,
specks of staleness and freshness.

The exact and exacting notice of such detail is one of the great gifts Kinsella proves in his poetry, bringing the reader deeply into the poem where the experience is shared, and shared in its immaculate and original texturing. The thunder sounds again, 'time not quite stopped'. The egg begins to fall towards the shore. No great event, no integument-shattering explosion, but a small smashing of an ordinary egg, while the old woman's comment is 'There's plenty more where that came from!' Whether or not the reader wants to find some rich philosophies behind this moment held and retold is immaterial: the point is in the actual moment between the egg's appearance and its fall. And this is the epiphany, and this is its effect on the young watcher:

I feed upon it still, as you see;
there is no end to that which,
not understood, may yet be noted
and hoarded in the imagination,
in the yolk of one's being, so to speak,
there to undergo its (quite animal) growth,
dividing blindly,
twitching, packed with will,
searching in its own tissue
for the structure
in which it may wake.
Something that had – clenched
in its cave – not been

now was: an egg of being.
Through what seemed a whole year it fell
– as it still falls, for me,
solid and light, the red gold beating
in its silvery womb,
alive as the yolk and white
of my eye; as it will continue
to fall, probably, until I die,
through the vast indifferent spaces
with which I am empty.

One of the results of a failure of imagination is the loss of a sense of structure in life, a loss of order, leading a person, or indeed a nation, to blunder forward in the pursuit of whatever bauble hovers brilliantly at eye level. Taking the moments of epiphany, as Thomas Kinsella has it, and rooting through their hoarding for meaning, offers the possibility of structure, and of order. Kinsella's poetry demonstrates how the imagination, seriously impelled, is the opposite of fantasy and has to be based on what is real. If we find a structure in life composed of the epiphanies that surface to us, then that very structure will greatly enrich that life. If, however, the images by which we live are imposed from without, then all sorts of evil will result. Let me mention only the positioning of imagined weapons of mass destruction before the eyes of the world when George Bush was lining up to invade Iraq. And on a smaller scale, the images set upon us by TV advertising, to make us buy useless and sometimes dangerous products we simply cannot live without.

I do not wish to appear merely severe and moralistic in my appeal for faith in the hoard of the imagination. But I will not withdraw the sense of importance that I place on its use. So let me push, without further apology, deeper still. In our time, as is quite evident, the word 'religion', the word 'God', the word 'Devil' – all of these have been sidelined lest they give rise to unrelieved mockery of the one who uses them. Czeslaw Milosz quotes graffitti written up on a wall somewhere in California: 'God is Dead – Nietzsche; (and, in another hand underneath)

Nietzsche is dead – God.' Which brings me around to language, the manipulation of words, indeed the power of unadulterated words. Imagination alone, and most often in poetry, will relish the principle of contradiction inherent in our use of language as vital to development, leading to fullness; and let me focus on one such productive contradiction: the absent God is the present God – in the poetry of R. S. Thomas.

Thomas takes you by the lapel so you need to answer: 'By thy long grey beard and glittering eye now wherefore stoppest thou me?' This is a wholly legitimate and necessary question, and one not asked often enough. If it is asked of the poem, and if the poem answers, then a sadder and a wiser man you will wake the following morn. Therefore, in writing poetry, there is a double responsibility: the completion of the writer's task is a readership, but a small one, or sometimes only one's replying self, ought to suffice. Poetry is the taking of the world as it is, in its physical and absorbed detail, and placing the spirit within it, as in a clear-glass fish-bowl, for amazement, enjoyment, and order. It is a seeing beyond the actual, but through the medium of the actual, to what appears suddenly luminous and important, an intuition of the infinite significance of the ordinary everyday world, a sense of our oneness with all of creation, in its individual parts and in its wholeness.

I had the great but alloyed pleasure of bringing the late and wonderful poet R. S. Thomas on a day trip out of Dublin. I had admired the work for years, its power and range, its deeply probing, almost fanatical and tetchy honesty, bringing with it, for me, a sense that I would be terrified in that man's presence. The contrary was the case, as I should have guessed. He chatted easily, he put me at my ease. I tried to show him the glories of Newgrange but he would not get out of the car, merely nodding his head from a distance at our national wonder. What he wanted was to talk, to be with another person, to probe, to listen, to discuss. He envied me what he saw as Ireland's freedom from all things English, and I was aware of his reputation at Eisteddfods, where he could stand up and urge his Welsh compatriots to cast the English out of all Welsh fields.

In his introduction to the *Faber Selected Poems of George Herbert*, Thomas says: 'The poet invents the metaphor, and the Christian lives it.' He quotes Simone Weil: 'Every true artist has had real, direct, and immediate contact with the beauty of the world, contact that is of the nature of a sacrament.' He went as priest to live among the Welsh hills, hoping to find this awareness of sacrament, and by writing about the lives of such people, to rail against the destruction in our world of the sense of sacrament. He is disappointed; what he found among the hill farmers was a grossness and earthiness he was not prepared for, an instinct for survival that ignored the sacramental richness of the acres they had to farm. Here is part of his poem, *The Moor*, where he relishes the sacramental nature of the landscape:

It was like a church to me.
I entered it on soft foot,
Breath held like a cap in the hand.
…
There were no prayers said. But stillness
Of the heart's passions – that was praise
Enough; and the mind's cession
Of its kingdom.

But the relish of isolation is not enough for a priest or pastor. He faced the people and found his peasant, as in an early poem where his prototype farmer, Iago Prytherch, works 'with a half-witted grin of satisfaction.'

And then at night see him fixed in his chair
Motionless, except where he leans to gob in the fire.
There is something frightening in the vacancy of his mind.

In his long poem, *The Minister*, written for the BBC, a minister arrives in 'the hill country at the moor's edge'; you can see Thomas himself in this description of the young minister:

My cheeks were pale and my shoulders bowed
With years of study, but my eyes glowed
With a deep, inner phthisic zeal,
For I was the lamp which the elders chose

To thaw the darkness that had congealed
About the hearts of the hill folk.

Not so easy as all that! The 'narrator' of the poem tells us:
They chose their pastors as they chose their horses
For hard work. But the last one died
Sooner than they expected; nothing sinister,
You understand, but just the natural
Breaking of the heart beneath a load
Unfit for horses. 'Ay, he's a good 'un,'
Job Davies had said; and Job was a master
Hand at choosing a nag or a pastor.

R. S. begins by wishing to bring the God he has come to know to the people under his care, but it is Thomas's God he arrives with, and it is Thomas's awareness, delicate sensibility, faith, love and a fierce imaginative power that tries to overcome the locals. Soon, he begins to falter:
I have failed after many seasons
To bring truth to birth,
And nature's simple equations
In the mind's precincts do not apply.

These hill farmers weave their dogged slow ways through the poems of R. S. Thomas, and what we are witness to is the loss of Thomas's faith in his power to move them. Gradually, living amongst them, he moves from a sense of contempt to one of awareness and acceptance of their harsh lot in life. He wonders how they can survive the pains they must necessarily undergo, in order to wrest a living from the harsh and non-sacramental earth. The honesty and self-awareness of this movement in the poet is in itself assuring, and proof of the powerful force of his imagination; from standing outside gazing in, he moves to understand them fully and to grieve on their behalf. He has grown aware of 'the slow poison and treachery of the seasons'. At the same time he cannot help but be influenced by this harshness and the hill farmer's ignorance and carelessness about the finer things, until he finds himself doubting the very God he set out to

offer them. He has lived in 'pain's landscape', he has knelt long
and listened for God, but heard only the bats' wings whispering
in the high rafters. His imaginative journey has led him to such a
sympathy and empathy with those he despised that in one
poem, *Absolution,* he can say:

Prytherch, man, can you forgive
From your stone altar on which the light's
Bread is broken at dusk and dawn
One who strafed you with thin scorn
From the cheap gallery of his mind?

He can see that the man's soul is made strong, not by faith in
God, but 'By the earth's incense, the wind's song.' Now it is the
minister who seeks forgiveness from the sinner. From here it is
only a matter of time for the priest poet to move towards self-
doubt, and from there towards a doubt about the very existence
of his God. So, let us move back imaginatively to that moor we
began with, that, you will remember, was like a church to him:
here is a much later poem, *Moorland:*

It is beautiful and still;
        the air rarefied
as the interior of a cathedral

expecting a presence. It is where, also,
        the harrier occurs,
materialising from nothing, snow-

soft, but with claws of fire,
        quartering the bare earth
for the prey that escapes it;

hovering over the incipient
        scream, here a moment, then
not here, like my belief in God.

Thomas's journey, spurred on by his imaginative sympathies
and his concerns for the sufferings of simple men, has been
mapped by the poems. This is, of course, a necessary simplific-
ation; there is much, much more in the work than this. But what

I am hoping to shadow is the movement of a life charted by means of language and image and set before us as an offering, a template almost, of the shifts of a being committed to the deepest impulses of life in our time. Out of the gift of imagination Thomas packages for his readers guidelines and signposts, all from the argument the poet carries on within himself and with his God. In this next poem where almost all hope in God's existence is lost, the old story of Rapunzel serves as foil.

Folk Tale
Prayers like gravel
        flung at the sky's
window, hoping to attract
            the loved one's
attention. But without
        visible plaits to let
down for the believer
            to climb up.
To what purpose open
        that far casement?
            I would
have refrained long since
        but that peering once
through my locked fingers
I thought that I detected
        the movement of a curtain.

If it is fair to say that a good poem, lifting itself off a recognised and recognisable earth, takes that earth with it and draws imaginative order and ordering from it, it may also be true to say that the whole work of a poet provides the reader with a wider, deeper and more cumulative ordering that is vital to our understanding of the world. Thomas comes to a moment when he envies the mindlessness of his once despised peasants, because the peasant consents to an absence that the priest cannot consent to. The poetry of R. S. Thomas is an effort to regain an understanding of his place in the ongoing creation, an effort to restore an organic unity between man and creation. He eventually sees the silence of the hill farmer as its own poetry, a poetry of acceptance. Then, by reading the gathered poems, we find ourselves taking up a sort of hall-of-mirrors stance, being aware of the artistry of Thomas's work, while sharing the experience, the epiphanies and, at the same time, being conscious of his and our need to transcend that experience. We are witnesses to an honesty and integrity of imaginative exploration that does not impose its will on the material of the earth, but rather moves from enlightenment to enlightenment without shirking the consequences of such epiphanies. We are grasped by the poet, we are told, indeed we are shown, his story, and we wake the morrow morning cooler and wiser folk. Thomas makes the inarticulate speak to us, by articulating it so well and we are back to Thomas Kinsella's articulation of a seemingly unimportant moment, and back to the ambiguity and irony of Donne's sense of sin and repentance. We are privileged witnesses and beneficiaries of the imagination in exquisite torsion.

I want to quit the poetry of R. S. Thomas by quoting from a lesser-known aspect of his work. This dogged, determined, articulate and questioning clergyman was also a writer of extremely fine and moving love poetry. That is for another day but for the moment here is such a love poem, emblematic of the power of a moment of epiphany, caught and held, treasured and consummately articulated:

> *No Time*
> She left me. What voice
> colder than the wind
> out of the grave said:
> 'It is over'? Impalpable,
> invisible, she comes
> to me still, as she would
> do, and I at my reading.
> There is a tremor
> of light, as of a bird crossing
> the sun's path, and I look

up in recognition
of a presence in absence.
Not a word, not a sound,
as she goes her way,
but a scent lingering
which is that of time immolating
itself in love's fire.

'I look up in recognition of a presence in absence': a phrase
that brings us back to Kinsella's *Hen Woman* and the capture of a
moment of epiphany. There is no compulsion here to write about
the 'great events', the wars and horrors, the inhumanity and cor-
porate greed we are aware of. Czeslaw Milosz writes of the horrors of Auschwitz and the ongoing efforts of the human heart to
mask its brutal urgings and then goes on to say, with a nod towards Adorno's phrase, that 'gentle verses' though they be written in the midst of horrors 'declare themselves for life'. In this
way, poems of lyrical grace written about swans or roses or croc-
uses, about hens or hill farmers or one's own sense of sin, declare
themselves as anti-war. Each lyric produced and published may
be placed on that great weighing-scales of justice and peace, the
other side presently heavily loaded with humanity's disgrace.

The loss of imaginative life in a nation signals the loss of joy
and involvement, it signals the failure of a person or a people to
see through the things of the world to what lies behind them; for
the joyless, each object, each event, remains simply what it is, an
object, or an event; the epiphany of a poem offers an alternative
to the observed world, for we see and touch only the epidermis,
poetry brings us through to the skeleton where we may see the
structure of our living, our ills or our health, our sideways trajec-
tory or our wellbeing.

Let me end with an epiphany of my own, a small poem that
takes Jacob's famous dream of angels ascending and descending
the ladder fixed between earth and heaven, and that adds to it a
small matter of the medieval hearkening to the music of the
spheres; all of this coming from a small moment in the Leitrim
countryside:

Canticle

Sometimes when you walk down to the red gate,
hearing the scrape-music of your shoes across gravel,
a yellow moon will lift over the hill;
you swing the gate shut and lean on the topmost bar
as if something has been accomplished in the world;
a night wind mistles through the poplar leaves
and all the noise of the universe stills
to an oboe hum, the given note of a perfect
music; there is a vast sky wholly dedicated
to the stars and you know, with certainty,
that all the dead are out, up there, in one
holiday flotilla, and that they celebrate
the fact of a red gate and a yellow moon
that tunes their instruments with you to the symphony.

Full of Broken Things

Charlotte Mew (1859-1928)

Here is one of the forgotten poets! Charlotte was born and lived in central London all her life. Her father's death left her, with her mother and sister, in financial difficulties; two of her siblings were mentally ill and living in care. Charlotte and her sister, Anne, made a pact never to marry in case they might pass on to their own children this insanity in the family. Many of Charlotte's poems refer, naturally, to insanity. She published poems, stories and articles here and there and was eventually persuaded to publish a volume of poems, *The Farmer's Bride*, in 1915; many of the leading writers at the time welcomed it. In 1923 she was given a civil list pension on the recommendation of, among others, Thomas Hardy. This eased her financial problems but she did not achieve the lever of fame she hoped for in her lifetime. Clearly she is still quite neglected. Her mother died in 1923 and she and her sister lived alone. Charlotte committed suicide in 1928, soon after the death of her sister. Suffering and a Job-like cry to God run through her work; a sense of sin and suffering that she considered undeserved shoots across the poems. The note of rebellion in her poetry gives it a special piquancy. In our day and age her voice ought to appeal more widely than it has hitherto done.

A Question
If Christ was crucified – Ah! God, are we
    Not scourged, tormented, mocked and called to pay
    The sin of ages in our little day –
Has man no crown of thorns, no Calvary,
Though Christ has tasted of his agony?
    We knew no Eden and the poisoned fruit
    We did not pluck, yet from the bitter root
We sprang, maimed branches of iniquity.

Have we who share the heritage accurst
 Wrought nothing? Tainted to the end of time,
The last frail souls still suffer for the first
 Blind victims of an everlasting crime.
Ask of the Crucified, Who hangs enthroned,
If man – oh! God, man too has not atoned!

Not for that City
Not for that city of the level sun,
 Its golden streets and glittering gates ablaze –
 The shadeless, sleepless city of white days,
White nights, or nights and days that are as one –
We weary, when all is said, all thought, all done,
 We strain our eyes beyond this dusk to see
 What, from the threshold of eternity
We shall step into. No, I think we shun
The splendour of that everlasting glare,
 The clamour of that never-ending song.
 And if for anything we greatly long,
It is for some remote and quiet stair
 Which winds to silence and a space of sleep
 Too sound for waking and for dreams too deep.

D. H. Lawrence (1885-1930)

The Hands of God
It is a fearful thing to fall into the hands of the living God.
But it is a much more fearful thing to fall out of them.

Did Lucifer fall through knowledge?
Oh then, pity him, pity him that plunge!

Save me, O God, from falling into the ungodly knowledge
of myself as I am without God.
Let me never know, O God
let me never know what I am or should be
when I have fallen out of your hands, the hands of the living God.

That awful and sickening endless sinking, sinking
through the slow, corruptive levels of disintegrative knowledge
when the self has fallen from the hands of God,
and sinks, seething and sinking, corrupt
and sinking still, in depth after depth of disintegrative
    consciousness
sinking in the endless undoing, the awful katabolism into the
    abyss!
even of the soul, fallen from the hands of God!

Save me from that, O God!
Let me never know myself apart from the living God!

The Church
If I was a member of the Church of Rome
I should advocate reform:
the marriage of priests
the priests to wear rose-colour or magenta in the streets
to teach the Resurrection in the flesh
to start the year on Easter Sunday
to add the mystery of Joy-in-Resurrection to the Mass
to inculcate the new conception of the Risen Man.

In Dogged Loyalty

Pádraig J. Daly

Pádraig J. Daly offers the most sustained attempt at serious religious poetry in Ireland. His poetry begins with easy nostalgia for that innocent land we knew in our youth, when Roman Catholic Ireland moved like a Titanic through untroubled waters. Daly's work, however, moves quickly into the Augustinian concept that all our living is praise of God. But Luther, too, was an Augustinian and quickly his spirit enters Daly's work, subjecting his own life to examination.

In Daly's work, the interior desert imagery and the drudgery of living before an absent God make their first, startling appearance in Irish poetry. The language becomes sparer, the immediacy and closeness of the experience are conveyed quickly and with the accuracy of anguish.

There follows a series of poems hovering about the Merton ideal of productive silence and retreat where the Christ may be found again, and out of this silence words may flow with greater sound and fury. The natural response is to withdraw, to hide, but in a priest eager to serve others, a further response is needed. There comes a period of anger against this absent God. Anger, frustration, emptiness; is silence an adequate response? And where does the poet move from here?

Pádraig J. Daly was born in Dungarvan, Co Waterford, in 1943. He entered the Augustinian order and studied in Ireland and in Rome. He has worked as a priest in Dublin and in New Ross, Co Wexford. He has published several collections of poetry, amongst them *Nowhere But in Praise* (Profile Press 1978), *A Celibate Affair* (Aquila 1984), *Out of Silence* (Dedalus 1993), *The Voice of the Hare* (Dedalus 1997) and *The Last Dreamers, New & Selected Poems,* (Dedalus 1999). A further collection, *The Other Sea,* appeared from Dedalus in 2003. So there has been a steady stream of work from this priest poet, work that has moved on a downward curve in terms of trust and hope, and on an upward curve in terms of language, form and imagery.

It is the constants in the work, and the development of an individual voice and life through poetry, that interest me here. From the beginning there has been an eye on locale, an acute awareness of the physical world, captured always with an engaging sympathy: speaking of the Irish Famine in a poem called *Na Prátaí Dubha*, for instance, he writes:

Each day handcarts came through the town
To carry out the corpses.
Some were buried alive,
Taken up soundless from the roadway;
There was no energy for tears.

Nor was there ever any fudging or sentimentality in his view
    of things;

They moved purposefully among the rocks
In heavy greatcoats
Like huge primeval crustaceans.

They were not the happy poor.
(Family)

Very early in the work the Augustinian note is struck, a belief that everything in the world exists to praise God.

Man cannot evade You:
Every wary mouse,
The ant that builds and climbs,

Each small limpet on a rock,
The waters sucked noisily
Through stones on the shore,

The sleek and watery cormorant
Compel him
To shout You out ...

And nowhere but in praise
Can quark or atom
Or any fraction else of mass

Find peace.
(*Augustine: Letter to God*)

This poetry survives because of its music and the accuracy of
its observation, not because of its content which resorts so often
simply to statement. The voice is unique; the lines move with a
sense of breathing, slowly, capturing a mood of awed certainty;
the language is quite simply honed to perfection, 'sleek and watery cormorant', 'or any fraction else of mass'. In many ways,
here we have an early George Herbert, relishing the world about
him, and relishing it in terms of the music of poetry and the lifting of the heart towards God. Here it is the priest speaking, conscious of God, conscious too of the grace and promise that faith
in a loving God can bring. Only when the deeply personal note
is allowed in are we aware of any possible darkness in this pic-
ture.

Sagart I
In many ways you're like an old man. Perhaps
You walk alone more than most people twice your age.
You notice each change of weather, the drift
Of smoke to sky. There is a certain decorum
You follow in your dress, the way you comb your hair.

You have many acquaintances, few friends;
Besides your unreplying God you have no confidant.
Nevertheless you lift your hat to all. Old ladies
Especially will seek you out, sometimes a sinner.
You are guest at many celebrations, a must at birth or death.

Sometimes you wonder whether this is how God intended it.

It is my contention that great religious poetry appears only
when the individual heart and experience of the poet are faced
straight on; what smacks of proselytising in any way, tends to
alienate the reader and move language and shape into artificial

ways. *Sagart I* is an achieved poem because the music, the words, the long slow lines, all move deftly with the sentiment, the experienced matter of the poem. The music of the second line, for instance, with its open 'o' sounds, the strong vowels of 'walk' and 'twice' and 'age', sing effortlessly, but sing they do; the line itself moves with a stepping, walking cadence that is quite remarkable. Something like T. S. Eliot, something like Thomas Kinsella, Pádraig J. Daly works with a quiet music that is eminently charming and distinctly difficult to emulate.

Daly's love of Italy and things Italian also appears early on in his work. Coming from the damp and dark of a corner of the south-east of Ireland, perhaps the light and warmth, the energy and noise of the living there, took his fancy. As a young seminarian he studied for a number of years in Rome and learned Italian; indeed, one of the great Italian poets of her generation, Margherita Guidacci, translated a selection of Daly's poems into Italian, a book published in Rome in 1981. Daly himself has translated the poetry of Edoardo Sanguineti and Paolo Ruffilli into English. Italy, for him, has been no sunshine resort experience, but has touched him deeply. The early poems respond here, too, with a sense of awe and a call simply to praise:

So we found a birreria with sunshades outside
And its doorway framing all the valley.
Someone began to name the distant villages:
Cave, Olevano, Genazzano, Guadagnolo.

And I spoke a poem in my mind:
Schoolchildren chased geese across it
And I could not tie the dancing sunlight
Down or the beer's frothing.
(*Italian Journey*)

Praise often becomes a simple revelling in the things of the earth; Daly views children and animals in this light. Children break open watermains on a city hill to exult in the splashing water and this is like breaking 'great corners out of the darkness'. (*John Street Hill*)

They tie ropes round lamp-posts
And swing till nothing is solid
Or distant or fearful anymore.
(*Vicar Street Flats*)

A poem like *Among the Nettles* relishes the natural objects the
poet encounters; it is again the simple accuracy of the language
of observation here that gives the statements their value:

On quiet hillsides families of foxes
Sport at evening
Where green pines slice the sun.

The simple things are done well, and are not intrusive: the
vowel sound of 'quiet' repeated in 'hillsides' and again in 'pines
slice', so holding this stanza musically together; the 's' sounds
everywhere suggesting the sport, the alliteration of 'families of
foxes' suggestive of the togetherness of the animals. All is well,
and all manner of things appear well, and God is in his heaven ...

In 1984, Pádraig Daly published his collection *A Celibate
Affair*. The title itself ought to alert the reader to something
strange and new in the book. Daly begins by taking a much closer
look at the Jesus who had been simply a matter of praising up to
now. A new slowness and maturity begin to enter the poems. It
may well be that the isolation and loneliness that formed the
mood for the earlier *Sagart* poems had taken a stronger hold on
the maturing priest, who began to feel that the Christ, too, had
led a similar, almost 'outcast' life. In an earlier poem, *Problem*, he
had written, 'But I am blind still to the Jew / My life traipses
after'. This trudging after Jesus, this sense of tagging along,
needs to be clarified and strengthened if one is to stay close to
one's priestly vocation. *A Celibate Affair* sets up an arid stage on
which figures pass with a doggedness and determination that
are superbly caught in the desert imagery:

Animal after animal,
Huge relentless camels,
The children in light dresses running to keep pace.

The scenery is one of 'treacherous passes ... rock-strewn roads ... steep cliff-faces.
But always they must move;
And still they move.

This journeying, this shifting always forward of a Bedouin-like tribe of people, moves forward out of an inner necessity 'As if ahead somewhere were destination; / And somewhere stillness'. It is this 'as if' that throws even the priestly vocation into some doubt, some questioning. We are thus prepared for the next poem, which I want to quote in full:

Encounter
Monotony of sun
On sand and scrub,
A place of wild beasts
And long shadows;

At last he comes
To green and olivegroves,
Vineyards,
Houses climbing beyond walls
Along a hillside.

Here the tempter waits,
Full of candour,
Offering for easy sale
All the green kingdoms of the world.

And he,
Though gaunt from fasting,
Needing rest,

Some perfect star
Seen a lifetime back
Determining him,

Passes slowly by.

This is the figure of Jesus testing his own calling in the desert, drawing up out of the depths of his belief some original, promis-

ing motive for his fasting, his choosing the desert rather than the
green paths. We have moved on a great distance from the ease of
Augustine's songs of praise, to a sparer view of the natural
world, and to a harsher view of the interior spirit. 'A place of
wild beasts / And long shadows', has replaced the more ful-
some language of, for instance, *Tertullian on Prayer*:

The red cow
Coming from her stall
Looks up, moves forward,
Bellowing praise.

Without questioning the validity of the language or the
mood of either the earlier poetry, or of this middle ground, one
finds that the poems are already shadowing forth an interior
journey that is marked out in exceptionally honest and moving
terms. And in another poem in *A Celibate Affair*, the priest who
finds himself standing outside ordinary humanity in an effort to
raise his own and others' souls to God, finds himself even more
isolated when viewing a wedding party; here the imagery of an
interior desert, of the world in its bellowing of praise to God,
and of one standing apart from all of that, finds a unity and
wholeness that barely skirt desperation. Watching the wedding
party at evening, with the sky a beautiful red and orange glow,
the observer (who was probably the minister at the joining together of two young people) writes:

I find no image here:
My mind walks on deserts still,
Empty spaces beyond the city
With stones thrown roughly about, jagged edged.

A man bent over rock, become rock.

What is there left to a human being in such a situation? The
contemplation of man in his bleakest parts, and ... silence! There
is a short series of poems that speak of prisoners, and the guards
that suffer them. 'There is no hope here but to wait, / Nothing to
be expected.' The prisoners: 'We are paradigms of some enormous failure.' And what of the guards? 'The greatest danger

comes / When you carry your underworld back out'. An awareness of the depths of human misery (and a priest working in a
city parish, in a deprived area of that city, is very aware of
human misery) taints one's view of the beauty of natural things.
The poetry, while maintaining its linguistic music and accuracy,
and the line lengths of breathing and mood, with a definite mastery, is beginning to touch hurtful depths.

In this context Pádraig J. Daly published his next collection,
Out of Silence, (1993) and its guiding genius is Thomas Merton.
Although this is a benign presence in the work, there is in it, too,
a vague suggestion of sterility. In one poem, *Pentimento*, a note
of menace is struck for the first time in Daly's work, and the
menace comes not from human antagonisms but from God's
new indifference to the beings he has created.

He created emptiness first;
Then threw the world out like wool
To dangle amid the planets.

'Dangle' does not suggest much care, nor does 'threw'. He
created animals, too, and man, but the latter was 'bound by clay
and death and foolishness.'

Sitting back, he laughed;
While men and women
Built draughty palaces.

We have moved a very great distance indeed from the hymn
of praise the creation is to lift to its creator. Worse, this God begins to be seen as not really involved in human living: 'We cry
out; / But if he hears, / He moves away from our voices'.
Countering this sense of foreboding are figures like Merton and
St Thérèse; the latter is, of course, the saint of small things, of
isolation, of a dogged loyalty to her beliefs;

And in her room at night,
She shivered at the thought of God growing strange
And a death as final as the death of stars.

What, then, is left? Silence? Further hints of menace and
awareness of human suffering recur throughout this collection;

there is a terrifying image of people on a cattle train in 1943, the menace real, the slaughter impending: 'Never before was murder so innocently done.' Another poem, *Apocalyptic*, touches on the horror man himself has threatened on his world in the form of a nuclear holocaust. What, then, of silence? It may, at first, seem to be an option, as when, remembering his dead father he can say, 'Your silence is full of signals.' This is memory, the memory of togetherness and of love.

What is to be said about silence
Except that it is:
And you sought it out diligently in your woods,
Living alone with your books,
In the company of birds.

This, from *Thomas Merton*. There is a glow of envy about the poem, and yet there is also an awareness of sterility.

And there is little you can send us out of your silence
Except to say that it is:
And it cries out louder than our clamour.

That last line appears, in the context of the poem, rather gratuitous, unearned from the earlier stanzas of the poem, yet the presence of that line is a willed effort to avoid the acceptance that silence leads merely to emptiness, 'in the company of birds'. There is, then, an undoubted doggedness underlying these poems, a loyalty to what has been believed in with such joy and firmness in earlier work, shot through, however, with a growing sense of loss and dread.

All of these strands come together in some of the most powerful religious poems written by a committed believer in this country, in a 1997 collection, *The Voice of the Hare*. It is this collection that bursts from the poet with an (at last) unrestrained fury at the sense of betrayal that human suffering portrays. Gone is the possibility of simple praise; this will not do any more. Gone is the simple statement of God's glory, and of humanity's sacred destiny; such unquestioning faith will not suffice any longer. But the priest's deeply committed care and humanity respond, not to a great cosmic calamity, nor to any national disaster, but to a small and individual pain, the small and individual things of life having already been focused on all through the poetry. And God?

Nothing disturbs him.

> He does not care any longer
> Whether we eat the fruit or not.
> *(He)*

This is the servant of God and man, who has done his utmost in care and hope, and who finds that the apparent cheat in all of this is God himself. In a most stark and powerful poem, *Complaint*, all the previous poetry is turned on its head; a depth of sorrow and bleakness is reached, and the sense of a personal God responding to a personal plea, becomes a cry of rage against the unresponsive 'Sir'. To name somebody is to suggest a certain degree of closeness and friendship; the coldness and distance of this repeated 'Sir', in this context, is deeply moving. Here is the poem:

> I will tell you, Sir, about a woman of yours,
> Who suddenly had all her trust removed
> And turned to the wall and died.
>
> I remember how she would sing of your love,
> Rejoice in your tiniest favour;
> The scented jonquils,
>
> The flowering currant bush,
> The wet clay
> Spoke to her unerringly of benevolence.
>
> I remind you, Sir, of how, brought low,
> She cowered like a tinker's dog,
> Her hope gone, her skin loose around her bones.
>
> Where were you, Sir, when she called out to you?
> And where was the love that height nor depth
> Nor any mortal thing can overcome?

Does it please you, Sir, that your people's voice
Is the voice of the hare torn between the hounds?

The depth of care, frustration and anger contained in this
poem is immense. On its own the poem is one of the finest written in the human questioning of a benign God, of a Providence.
But given all the fine work that has gone before, the rich texture
of the poems, the music of language, the gentle and firm breath-
movement of the lines, this poem is even more of a shock and a
disturbance. If silence leaves only a sense of sterility, then the
rage that is put into the questioning of what had been held for
truth, may be a way out. But for the priest, what can this do? If
the priest frames his faith in such terrible questions, how can he
then speak with comfort to his people?

I watch one I have grown to love,
Beautiful as the wind, languish;
And I flounder in the grief around her ...

Your people mutter bitterly against you;
How can I carry them?
(Sorrow)

There is another poem that sums up a life, a faith, a hope and
a loss of strength:

The Last Dreamers
We began in bright certainty:
Your will was a master plan
Lying open before us.

Sunlight blessed us,
Fields of birds sang for us,
Rainfall was your kindness tangible.

But our dream was flawed;
And we hold it now,
Not in ecstasy but in dogged loyalty,

Waving our tattered flags after the war,
Helping the wounded across the desert.

A great many of the images used in the earlier work reappear, though changed, changed utterly. Perhaps this is the lowest point to which this particular poet has sunk, in terms of his own capacity for joy, hope and faith. But it is a high point in his work, the most convincing poetry, the most piercing imagery and language. Here Daly has touched on the same cold flame that drove the poems of the later R. S. Thomas, this sense of an absent, worse, an uncaring God. And where can he go from here? The rest of this collection, *The Voice of the Hare*, is taken up with things a little distant from the instant pain that these poems touch on, memories of relatives and friends. It is a kind of cooling down period, a gathering of energies, a smoothing of crumpled sheets. Will it lead anywhere? Will it help?

In 2003 Pádraig J. Daly published another collection, *The Other Sea*. What is evident at once is a new 'outsideness', the poetry touching on places like Africa and allowing the strangeness there to take care of the imaginative side of the poetry. Daly has always been translating and reworking the canon of poetry in Gaelic and this, too, begins to take a stronger place in his imaginative life. There is, perhaps, a sense of calm, almost of a calm that has gone beyond hope, a waiting for God to manifest himself again, in some way not yet anticipated or imagined.

The List
The list of those who loved us
And are gone
Grows longer.

Where can we find the will
To let ourselves be loved,
To love again?

Like trees that show a Winter carapace,
Like bulbs and seeds at rest,
We bide till light returns.

Here is a sort of desperate quietism, a patience that has gone so far beyond hope that little is left. And still the poetry retains those qualities that give Daly's work its uniqueness: that breathing length of line, those words like 'carapace' and 'bide' that are surprising in themselves yet wholly right. Poems of memory and nostalgia take their places in this collection but what appears of most importance is that echo of R. S. Thomas, that acceptance that perhaps our God exists but he has taken himself away from us and cannot be found, not even intuited, yet must be accepted.

Real God
Once we were in a grey country
With a grey and dismal God.

Now we are in a bright country
With a bright, flourescent God.

But Real God hides
In unfathomable light.

One may travel a great journey with Pádraig J. Daly, a journey that shifts from the outer world of lovely things to a dark interior world where grey mists prevail. Those mists persist. But so does that doggedness in belief that he set out with. And about mid-way through this latest collection, that loyalty surfaces again. Perhaps we have come through! Though now the thought patterns are more complex, and the language more concerned, yet the power of his observation and the vigour of the language have brought about a new vision of the impossible glory of a triune God:

Trinity
The sea by itself is water merely:
Its miracle is in its beating against the shore,
Spreading out across flat sands,

Shifting shingle and stone,
Flowing over piers and jetties,
Halting before rock

And falling backward on itself to try again,
Leaping high in the storm,
Quietly attacking the very base of land.

And God and God and God are love merely
Until they find foolish us
To take love's overflow.

Perhaps the last three lines are willed lines, but then faith, after going through all the doubts and dismays a genuinely caring life goes through, comes down to an act of will, a choice, a decision to opt for what may well be the only hope that gives meaning to our lives. We are left with loyalty, a dogged loyalty, but that loyalty, hard-earned, is perhaps the most true approach to religious faith, a loyalty urged and lived by people like Simone Weil. But the poetry is achieved, moving with a flow and certainty to those last lines, building up an image and sound pattern that earn the music of that last statement. The long 'e' sound of that first line, is echoed in the third last line by the repetition of the word God and is re-echoed in the vowel of 'love'; and note those sound patterns that lead to the very final word, 'overflow': 'flat sands', the 's' music of the fourth line, the short and halted sixth line with its long and back-flowing seventh, and that forceful line that leads into the final triplet. And there are the exciting words that hit the mark so well, 'the very base of land', 'foolish us', 'love's overflow.'

At the height of his linguistic and formal power, Pádraig J. Daly struck a rock that submerged his optimism and his certainties but gave us a poetry of real worth and strength. What he may well be undergoing right now is a form of recovery, of finding new ways towards that absent God that R. S. Thomas celebrated in a rush of powerful poems. What cannot recur is a simple celebration of the glories of creation, certainly not in a world where the apocalyptic disasters Daly has written of appear almost sure to be brought about by man's own foolishness and his incapacity for unconditional love. If Daly's God, if Augustine's

and Merton's and Thérèse of Lisieux's God, is to be rediscov-
ered, it must be in different terms, under the canopies of a differ-
ing imagery, in experiences that go beyond dreams and auto-
matic care, and in a language urgent with the newness of its
vision. It is one of the greatest joys a reader of poetry knows, to
be privileged to follow the developing patterns of a poet as vital
and meaningful as Pádraig J. Daly.

The Censorship of Indifference
or
The Demise of Poetry

I have laboured in the cabbage-garden of Irish poetry for many years, watching it move from dark rooms in the backs of pubs where the till's shrill whistles interrupted the flow of verse and where the poet was thankful for a pint as reward, to the development of *Poetry Ireland*, through the sure hands of Rory Brennan, Theo Dorgan and Joseph Woods, into a national and highly-respected institution. I have seen the end of the Dolmen Press and the flowering of new small houses of poetry publishers. It has been a slow and sometimes disheartening development, but poetry in Ireland has taken a high place in the consciousness of the nation. Or has it? It is boasted of in international circles; presidents quote bits and pieces of it in their speeches; institutions around the world honour the Irish poet. And yet, today, this appears to be a tinsel bell, an empty gourd, a glitzy show full of empty platitudes and sounding brass.

I have never found poetry so ignored in actuality as I do today.

I feel sad and strange to find myself offering a defence of poetry once more. Ireland seems to have lost that sense of its value that it boasts itself of holding onto for centuries. But before I can pray for the buoyant sense of poetry's worth to return to our country, let me state some of the reasons why it must hold that worth. Literature imposes an order on our experience, even those forms of literature that treat of disorder in a seemingly disordered way, like Beckett's work, like the later Joyce. The reproach offered to all forms of culture has been, and remains, that it does impose such an order, determining a map of meanings and symbols that creates a screen to hide the horror and disorder that is reality. Give us reality TV, is the cry; take away the unreal world of the imagination! If poetry speaks, by being poetry,

220

of the dignity of mankind, how we are created in God's image and likeness, if it speaks of beauty and truth and goodness, while wars and horrors abound at the same time, then it is poetry that appears to be offering a loud and cantankerous lie.

Homer in his epics outlined an order imposed on warring humans and warring gods. The *Iliad*, the *Odyssey*, while being huge tales of battles and conflict, suggest a reigning plan and ordering underneath the murdering and betrayals. The Bible offered a similar ordering of things. Between them they form the basis of European culture. When this ordering fell apart, irreparably as it appears, when the machine age found its legs and started to move, then God died, and European culture lost its hold. This truth surfaces over and over again because, over and over again, times of universal suffering do recur. In our time, a terrible form of nihilism once again screams its presence, creating a framework within which our culture stands and we are reminded of the works that surfaced during and after the Second World War, in Tadeusz Rozewicz for example, who took the great and magical Prospero and showed how his civilising powers failed abysmally to change the awful Caliban.

War continues to show up all the inadequacies in our living and places the greatest possible stress on our forms of culture and our power with language. Nine-eleven, the war in Iraq, the Israeli-Palestinian conquest, and above all, perhaps, the most recent and unacceptable obscenities of Fallujah, leave us all with a sense of staining, and of helplessness. If noble intentions were enough, we would have a magnificent literature to counter war, but it has been learned that coldness and distance are required to form a literature, while the outpourings of fact and witness often remain in the realm of reportage. This, of course, is wholly valid in itself for such works may well serve as testament, and are salutary, whereas a literature born of retrospection may serve as monument to our experiences of elemental horror.

All our literatures, our philosophies, our religions, are built with the bricks and mortar of language and therefore the purity and truth of words remain crucial to our wellbeing. If the general sense of a loss of confidence in literature – demonstrated by the indifference of the greater part of humanity to poetry and 'serious' or 'literary' fiction – has resulted in a two-tiered humanity, then perhaps literature remains in a realm apart and distinctly ineffective. And to this must be added the comparatively recent phenomenon (recent because of the proliferation and power of mass media) where language has been stolen by people in power who have wrested some control over the media, and who manipulate words to suit their own agendas. Then a third tier of culture emerges and the 'common' man, pressed to believe he relishes a lower grade of literature, continues to lose all his autonomy as an individual, while the more educated and discerning reader or viewer finds herself at odds with government, out on a limb, lost to both power and audience.

Already in the twenty-first century there are disasters and realities that language cannot encompass: Zimbabwe, Afghanistan, the 'natural disaster' of the tsunami in South-East Asia – many more; the only way to come at such vast events is to approach them at an angle, by a roundabout way, reflecting an individual's actual experience, a personal subjectivity. After the Holocaust, Adorno said, and we all know the phrase, poetry is not possible. Yet poetry continues to be written and often now it may take the form of Job's cry of despair that goes on to become the cry of the survivor. Humanity is in the process of becoming; objects do not become, they are: the stone, the goat, the rhododendron; it is the becoming that is difficult. In the process of this becoming there is a line beyond which nothing but silence exists and that is the line that poetry must brush up against, a line that the greatest poetry peers beyond.

In the approach to the subject and fact of contemporary warfare, poetry is constantly shoving up against that line. Perhaps the surest way to peer over, is to do so in the circumventive way suggested, by touching on individual experiences and writings. The act of writing will change depending on the writer's awareness of actual background reality surrounding him or her. And today's realities? The frailty of our systems of government, of our systems of values, the immensity of the war machine wielded by a powerful few, the use of language as a weapon of deceit. In our time nothing is guaranteed.

In Ireland, if our culture of caring for strangers, of welcome, of donating to the poor of other countries, has rapidly been giving way to a culture of business values (or lack of them), towards economic success, profit, ego: if our bookshops will not stock poetry volumes because they can sell only a handful of copies and that slowly, while they stock, display and sell thousands of copies of forest-destroying, jelly-and-custard trash fiction: if the religious imagination finds itself sidelined, ignored, mocked into a locked outhouse to give way to aggressive and emphatic scientific and technological takeovers, then it is clear that our humanness is in dire trouble. This falling away goes hand in hand with our turning our backs on Christianity. In our time religious art in all its forms is facing incredible, even aggressive, indifference. Tradition itself has become suspect.

If, then, the artist (the poet, say) is expected still to stand at the margins, has the margin now become what used to be the centre of our living? If the poet is to be a rebel, does he/she rebel on behalf of the traditional values of our culture, against modern business methods? Or does he/she take part in the ongoing rush to wealth by tailoring the work in order to sell, in order to make a living? Do we judge the value of a book of poetry by how much publicity hype it achieves and by how many copies are sold at a launching party? Or the painter by the number of thousands of euro paid for a painting on the opening evening? Has poetry been relegated to small intense groups in professors' rooms on the highest floors of our universities? It appears that the way for poetry is to become more and more esoteric and, accepting its role as outside the economic lifestyles, will it be asked to lie down and die? Or will it become more and more melodramatically demotic, hoping to find its place in some emporium of 'entertainment', along with television reality programmes, or blockbuster movies? Or does it become more 'engaged', hoping to struggle along with the great mass of people astonished at

how our world has devoted itself more and more fully to war
and pre-emptive strikes?

There is an economic globalisation which either extends
what we see happening around us in Ireland, or has become a
muddy and sucking hole into which Ireland has gladly fallen.
Yet there is – and perhaps it is in response to this globalisation –
a cultural entrenchment under way. In the area of poetry it
shows itself as an indifference to poetry in general, and to poetry
in translation in particular. If it is simply impossible to get volumes
of poetry onto the shelves of our bigger bookstores, it is utterly
hopeless to try and get these stores to take poetry in translation.
If only a minimum of newspapers and journals give reluctant
space to the reviewing of our home-produced volumes of poetry,
there is next-to-nothing done in the way of reviews of poetry in
translation. Perhaps as a consequence of our rush to cash we feel
it incumbent on us to ignore, in some perverted 'patriotic' way,
the possible value to be discovered in other cultures?

It is a commonplace to say that countries that have recently
suffered or are currently suffering some form of oppression or
dictatorship, look eagerly to poetry for spiritual sustenance and
uplift. I have been in Medellín in Colombia at a festival of poetry;
audiences for readings in many languages were impressive,
concluding with a shifting audience in an open-air auditorium
of between four and six thousand people, many of them staying
for the full four-hour performance. A great percentage of these
were young people, eager, enthusiastic and grateful. At an
evening of poetry in Skopje, Macedonia, during the summer of
2004, there was an audience standing near the old city bridge
and listening to poetry for several hours, again in many languages; the audience was estimated at two thousand, and the
event was televised live. On the other hand I have been to a festival in Bruges, where a bourgeois audience attended the opening
spectacular; these were well dressed people, mostly elderly, and
one got the impression that this was an occasion at which to be
seen. The later slog of poetry readings without wine and finger-
food receptions had nothing like so large an audience. I am not

saying that this is invalid; poetry survives both kinds of audience; what it may not survive is the lack of an audience. It is the censorship of indifference that is to be feared.

Where the culture fragments its traditional supports, then the individual can well feel outside the shifting cultural morass and become an even more marginal figure. The equilibrium is disturbed. Ireland in the 50s and 60s was far from being a perfect society, but everybody knew where he or she stood. As that society struggled to come to terms with the new, aggressive economies, the lyrical 'I' tended to become estranged. Witness how Kavanagh's sense of loss imploded in anger, Austin Clarke's in satire, Thomas Kinsella's into an ever-deepening exploration of the vulnerable self.

Poetry brings us back to the object, if it is good poetry, even if the subjective 'I' seems to dominate. Perhaps our times fail to view the object any more: the winter-flowering cherry in our suburban gardens, the snowberry in the country ditch, the marshalling magpies on our chimney-pots, the gangs of rooks heading home together after their day's predations. Growing aware of the earth about us again may well be part of the cure we need. Growing aware of the necessity for truth in language is also an essential element, and good poetry necessarily demands integrity in language, something we greatly miss today, particularly so in the commitments solemnly spoken by some of our public representatives.

You

Bring me ashore where you are
   that I may still be with you, and at rest.

Your name on my lips, with thankfulness,
   my name on yours, with love.

That I may live in light and know no terror of the dark;
   but that I live in light.

When I achieve quiet, when I am in attendance,
   be present to me, as I will be to you.

That I may hear you, like a lover, whisper yes –
   but that you whisper yes.

Be close to my life, my loves, as lost son to mother,
   as lost mother to son.
      But be close.

Come to me on days of heat with the cool breathing
   of white wine, on cold
   with the graced inebriation of red.
      But that you come.

That you hold me in a kindly hand
   but that you hold me.

Do not resent me when I fail
   and I fail, and I fail, and I fail.

That I may find the words.

That the words I find to name you
   may approach the condition of song.

That I may always love with the intensity of flowers
   but that I love,
      but that I always love.

John F. Deane